VICTORIAN MODERN

VICTORIAN MODERN

A Design Bible for the Victorian Home

with over 350 illustrations

JO LEEVERS
PHOTOGRAPHS BY **RACHAEL SMITH**

CONTENTS

6 INTRODUCTION

10 HALLWAYS

40 LIVING ROOMS

80 DINING ROOMS

108 KITCHENS

148 BEDROOMS

180 BATHROOMS

210 WORKSPACES

236 DIRECTORY & RESOURCES

238 INDEX

INTRODUCTION

ON P. 2
Acidic colours and personal collections in Lucinda Chambers's home.

ON P. 4
'Lyford Trellis', an uplifting pattern from Quadrille, wraps around Solange Azagury-Partridge's staircase.

OPPOSITE
In her house, Linda Allen hid storage behind dark panelling.

BELOW
Annabel White's home has been creatively reimagined to include this unusual staircase.

By accident and then by design, I've always lived in Victorian homes. I grew up in a flat in a 19th-century house in West London, then rented a variety of period homes, from a back-to-back terrace in Norwich to attic rooms in East London originally intended for servants. The first house I ever bought was a two-up, two-down, and I'm about to move from a Victorian semi to a city terrace. You get the picture.

But in each of these houses, I was always aware of how the original architecture had been adapted, with varying degrees of success. Through my work as an interiors writer, I then got to visit many more Victorian houses all around the UK, from grand mansions to rustic farmhouses, converted pubs to genteel seafront residences. Some felt very traditional; in others, the original character had been erased so efficiently you could have been standing in a crisp new build. I realized that the most interesting homes were those that rose to a specific challenge: how to create a modern home with personality within the frame of a Victorian house.

The reason why so many of us face this challenge is because the Victorian era – 1837 to 1901 – saw a building boom like no other, responding to industrialization and a widespread move to the cities. Over the course of the 19th century, the UK population grew from 8.9 million to over 41.5 million. By 1901, the year of Queen Victoria's death, over 17 per cent lived in London, while

cities such as Manchester, Liverpool, Leeds and Edinburgh had also grown rapidly.

While the working class tended to live near the factories, the emergent middle class were drawn to the new suburbs, where better-built terraces and semi-detached houses sprang up, served by railway lines and omnibus routes. A new commuter class was born, and the pressure was on to establish itself as respectable.

It soon emerged that one of the most effective ways to do this was through the home. Bare rooms signified poor taste, so every space was filled with the latest furniture, wallpaper and decorative objects, and there were plenty of bossy books on household management to instruct the newly-wed wife in what to buy. This desire to 'get the look' ran alongside a wider burgeoning interest in design, as witnessed by the Great Exhibition at the Crystal Palace in 1851. Meanwhile,

technological advances were bringing mass-produced objects – furniture to fabrics, tiles to carpets – within the reach of many.

But the overstuffed Victorian interior can also be seen as a reaction to a fast-changing society that lay just beyond the doorstep. Cities were seen as dens of iniquity and poverty; once the Victorian gentleman returned from work and entered his front door, sweet order was restored by the 'Angel in the House', his wife. The architecture of these homes reflected the rigid gender and class divides of the day. Floorplans, too, were all about keeping up appearances, with the front reception room acting as the house's public face, and cooking and washing hidden away at the back or in the basement, along with the servants.

In our modern homes, this approach has been almost totally reversed, with open-plan spaces that integrate cooking, eating and entertaining, and have a sense of light and flow. To accommodate this change, today's homeowners have had to come up with ingenious ways to incorporate contemporary living within a Victorian structure.

Photographer Rachael Smith and I set out to bring together the very best of these homes, from a tiny farmworker's cottage in Norfolk (p. 196), full of space-saving solutions, to an elegant villa in Ladbroke Grove (pp. 64, 104), which has been transformed with colour and architectural vision. We avoided houses that had lost their original character in the pursuit of modernity, and focused instead on those that inspire and add yet another layer to their ongoing stories.

Taking each room in turn – starting with hallways and ending with workspaces – we delve into the history of how it was originally used, helping to explain the architectural features – and quirks – of our inherited houses. The second half of each chapter brings us bang up to date, showcasing how leading interior designers, architects and creative owners have transformed their rooms with fresh ideas. Because while the Victorians saw decorating their homes as a way to conform, we are free to do the opposite – to create rooms that invigorate and express our individuality.

Welcome to the Victorian Modern home.

OPPOSITE ABOVE
'Tulip Midi' chairs by Pierre Paulin sit beneath a Murano glass chandelier in Suzanne Sharp's elegant dining room.

OPPOSITE
Rich colour contrasts breathe new life into Annie Sloan's home in Oxfordshire.

RIGHT
Mary Mulryan's former pub has been stripped back and revived with a contemporary eye.

HALLWAYS

In the affluent Victorian home, the hallway was all about creating a favourable first impression. Today, of course, we have far more freedom to express individual taste. There is also plenty of scope to adapt the original architecture to better suit modern life, from the addition of extra storage in a tight space to a large-scale renovation. Simpler changes in decor can also help make this transitional zone feel more connected to the rest of the house.

ON P. 10
Lush greenery complements the terracotta
tones of this back entrance to Juan de
Mayoralgo's house.

OPPOSITE
Interior designer Flora Soames lifted the
mood of this entrance hall with an orange
stair runner and a globe lantern.

BELOW
A range of ornate chandeliers in crystal
and engraved glass for the discerning
buyer. Silber & Fleming catalogue, 1881.

MAKING AN ENTRANCE

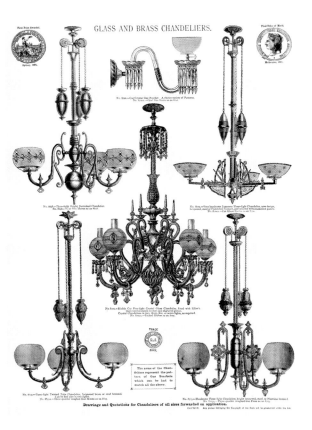

As the hallway provided the first glimpse of one's home,
Victorian homeowners tended to make their interiors as lavish
as they could afford, with the addition of patterned or textured
wallpaper below the dado rail, gilt-framed portraits above, or
a handsome hat stand. But it wasn't just about appearances: the
decorative elements outside the entrance also helped to subtly
reinforce a sense of privacy, with cast-iron gates, railings and
pillars emphasizing the home as a place of refuge from the
rapidly expanding city that lay beyond the front door.

The porch (sometimes followed by a vestibule) and hallway
provided ample opportunity for adding those all-important
flourishes. Stained glass was set into doors and smaller side
windows, adding colour, pattern and extra screening where
houses were built close together. Early designs incorporated
Gothic Revival motifs, before gradually giving way to gentler
botanical shapes, followed by stylized Art Nouveau designs
towards the end of the century.

In more imposing homes, glazed tiles also appeared on
the walls of porches, with pastoral scenes and floral motifs
proving particularly popular. Designs by William Morris and
William De Morgan were available only to the wealthy few, but
there were plenty of cheaper imitations available for those on
modest budgets.

Underfoot were encaustic or unglazed clay tiles, popularized
by Herbert Minton, a name that is still synonymous with
tiles. Minton rose to prominence in the 1840s as a result of
collaborations with the Gothic Revival architect A.W.N. Pugin
on ecclesiastical projects and the Palace of Westminster, but
his reputation was sealed with the commission to create tiled
floors for Osborne House, Queen Victoria and Prince Albert's
home on the Isle of Wight.

The Victorian home was a refuge from the confusing and rapidly expanding city that lay beyond the front door.

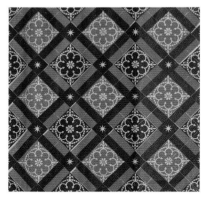

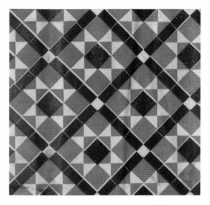

Minton's elaborate designs, which drew heavily on Gothic Revival motifs such as the fleur-de-lis and the trefoil, set the standard for paths, porches and hallways across the nation. Where encaustic tiles were too expensive, square clay tiles in plain red, brown and cream could be arranged into simple geometric patterns; examples of this thrifty practice remain in situ in many homes today.

Other decorative features, including midway arches, cornicing and plaster corbels, look impressive but did not always have a structural purpose. Some were fitted by canny builders who soon realized that mouldings bought from catalogues instantly made a standard semi-detached house look a cut above the rest, meaning they could charge a higher rent.

In houses where the main reception room was on the first floor, landings were regarded as equally important as the entrance hall – a tradition that is well worth reviving. These spaces can be furnished with favourite pieces or lined with bookshelves, and made to feel like rooms in their own right.

LEFT
Patterns for encaustic tiles from Maw & Co. catalogue, 1853.

OPPOSITE
Classic tiles in the home of Collette Vernon, who painted the original panelling to lighten the space.

THE MODERN HALLWAY

Contemporary updates of the Victorian hallway embrace colour, pattern and light to leave the gloom of the 19th century behind.

ABOVE
An ultra-modern staircase by BWArchitects sweeps through Annabel White's home.

OPPOSITE
A switch in colour takes a flight of stairs to the next level.

At first, the narrow hallway of a traditional Victorian terrace or semi-detached house – a long, skinny room with little natural light and punctuated by several doorways – presents a challenge for the modern homeowner. Yet these spaces can be adapted creatively, as can other layouts inherited from the era, from the square central hallway with rooms radiating off it to semis with the front entrance at the side, or houses with the front door opening directly into a reception room.

Freed from preconceptions about what a hallway 'should' look like, contemporary entranceways embrace colour, pattern and light to leave the gloom of the 19th century behind. Glamorous examples include Danielle Bux's home, where rich textures come together to create latter-day Hollywood luxury (p. 18), and Scarlett Gowing's house, where modern lighting and indulgent wallpapers inject modernity into a historic space (p. 26). Suzanne Sharp demonstrates how a vibrant paint shade can act as an instant mood-lifter (p. 28), and Chris Graves plays with softer hues and strong patterns (p. 32).

For a more dramatic overhaul, architects Michaelis Boyd have imaginatively transformed a previously dark hallway by inserting expanses of glazing and an entirely new staircase (p. 24). Creating a loft extension also entails fitting a new flight of stairs, but, as Alex and Mishari Al-Bader have discovered, this can be a chance to inject bold new colours (opposite).

CREATING AN OLD-SCHOOL GLAMOUR

In this house in Barnes, southwest London, key architectural elements have been subtly updated, striking a balance between modernity and the house's 19th-century roots. The doors and windows in the entrance vestibule have been fitted with a bespoke stained-glass design that has echoes of Victoriana, but picks up on the modern grey paint shade used on the woodwork, contrasting it with rectangles of pale yellow and a scattering of jewel-like circles.

The interior design was created for actor Danielle Bux and her former husband, broadcaster Gary Lineker, by Jo Berryman (see pp. 72, 88) and it remains a family home, well used by both owners and their children. Cinematic touches include a row of old theatre seats and even a red carpet, in the form of a bespoke carpet runner. Lighting adds to the glamorous feel, with a set of holophane lights and dainty stair lights.

BELOW LEFT
The vestibule glazing, made by local stained-glass company Robin Cooper, references past and present.

BELOW
Delicate lace patterns and an ornate radiator at the side window.

OPPOSITE
Brass downlights set at foot-level are triggered by a motion sensor.

OPPOSITE
Antique globe lights cast a gentle glow along the hallway.

BELOW
Vintage cinema seats fit below the dado, which is painted in a steely grey.

The original floorboards had suffered from wear and tear over the decades, and have been replaced with parquet flooring that runs throughout the ground floor. Danielle didn't want the new floor to look too perfect, however, so it has deliberately been allowed to become dotted with dents, scratches and divots to suit the vintage vibe of the house.

More gently historic details come in the form of a delicate lace curtain, which hangs at a side window, and extravagantly decorated radiators. Coats and jackets are kept in an area to the left of the staircase, hidden behind a thick velvet curtain in pink, a colour that is reflected onto the side wall of the alcove.

ABOVE
Panes in different textures, opacities and tones feel subtly modern.

OPPOSITE, TOP LEFT
Stained or obscured glass in side windows gave the Victorian hall added privacy.

OPPOSITE, TOP RIGHT
Vivid green wallpaper makes the colours of the stained glass in the front door pop.

OPPOSITE, BOTTOM LEFT
Black woodwork acts as a sharp, modern framework for extravagant patterns.

OPPOSITE, BOTTOM RIGHT
A sofa in mustard velvet echoes the pale tint of the panes in a back door.

STAINED GLASS

In the 18th century, front doors were generally solid wood panels, with a fanlight above the door as the only means of bringing natural light into a hallway (the front door of 10 Downing Street is a classic example), but advances in the manufacture of stained glass brought both light and colour into the Victorian hallway. This was a gift to the designers of the Arts and Crafts movement, who experimented with colours, shapes and imagery for their high-end clients. By the 1870s, less elaborate stained glass was also within the reach of ordinary homeowners, who could choose designs from catalogues.

If the original glazing in your front door has not survived, there are many specialist glass companies today that can restore sections of stained glass, or fit new panes in patterns and colours to provide a fresh take on Victorian designs. For the purist, looking for an original door in reclamation yards is an alternative route, but do ensure that you have an experienced carpenter on hand to hang it, as it would be rare to find a door that is a perfect fit.

LETTING IN THE LIGHT

This 1850s villa in Dartmouth Park, North London, has a suitably impressive façade and porch flanked by columns. Step inside, however, and it is immediately apparent that the Victorian architecture has been sensitively adapted for modern life. The four-storey house originally had a staircase at the rear, but a redesign by architects Michaelis Boyd included the installation of a new one in curving steel that is modern in design, yet feels authentic because of the materials used.

The risers and treads of the new staircase are clad in reclaimed timber, echoing the floorboards, and the underside is clad in light-reflecting tadelakt (a traditional Moroccan lime-based plaster), which is also used on the walls. The first turn incorporates a semi-circular landing, providing a bird's-eye view over the dining and living spaces thanks to glass walls. This innovative design also allows natural light to flow from a large skylight at the top of the house into the spaces below.

Interior designer Simone McEwan of Nice Projects incorporated unfussy classics into the hallway scheme, including a 'Snoopy' table lamp by Achille and Pier Giacomo Castiglioni for Flos and a console by Malgorzata Bany, with a pendant light by Rose Uniacke above. The result is a hallway that functions as the house's quiet core, linking and illuminating the spaces and setting the tone for the flowing architectural design.

ABOVE LEFT
Light flows down the staircase from a skylight and rear windows.

LEFT
Enlarged doorways on either side of the hallway contribute to a feeling of openness.

OPPOSITE
Partially glazed walls and internal windows connect the ground-floor spaces.

WARMING UP A HISTORIC SPACE

While narrow hallways are a feature of many urban Victorian homes, lack of space was not something interior designer Scarlett Gowing and her husband Josh had to contend with when they moved into this Grade II-listed house in East Sussex, built for a retired army officer in 1879 and later used as a school, a convalescent home and a rehabilitation centre. It was more a matter of occupying the vast spaces – particularly the 10 m (nearly 33 ft)-high hallway – and injecting fresh character by toning down the darker elements.

The parquet flooring was sanded back, a silk and wool rug added and walls covered with shimmery wallpaper from Dedar, all of which help to break up the expanse of wooden panelling. The chandeliers were designed by Scarlett herself, and furniture designs by Charles Pollock and Warren Platner for Knoll help to erase the house's institutional past. A soft wool runner on the stairs and swags of voluminous curtains on the landing show how the use of different textures can swiftly change the mood. By combining various shapes and styles, Scarlett has created a new harmony, resulting in a space that is fresh and exciting, and respects its Victorian roots.

OPPOSITE
On the landing, peach silk curtains bring out the beauty of the wood panelling.

BELOW LEFT
The front door opens into this vestibule, with glazed doors to the central hall beyond.

BELOW
An expanse of red institutional carpet once covered the parquet flooring. The sofa is vintage Ligne Roset.

CELEBRATING A BRILLIANT COLOUR

You would expect to find plenty of rugs and brilliant patterns in the home of Suzanne Sharp, founder of The Rug Company, but it's the uplifting shade of hot pink on the walls of the hallway that delivers impact. Suzanne's fearless use of colour continues with an orange-patterned rug, although the staircase runners lean towards monochrome. The runner leading up to the first-floor bedrooms – where the walls switch to a luminous blue – is in a classic pattern, while the one heading down to the basement level, where Suzanne has her work room, is in artisanal stripes.

Back on the ground floor, the wide hallway, which leads into the large dining room and kitchen, feels like a room in its own right thanks to the bold colour. Twin chairs, upholstered in candy-striped cotton, frame a useful alcove built into the wall during the renovation of this four-storey Victorian villa. It keeps the clutter of daily comings and goings organized, and houses a mini-library of guidebooks, both local and global, for guests to browse through. By colour-coding the hallway – a trick that continues on the landings of the other floors in the house – Suzanne has added dynamism to the overall interior design. It also announces, loud and clear, that this is a home that embraces colour and challenges expectations.

ABOVE RIGHT
A gleaming Tom Dixon pendant draws the eye upwards to the original cornicing.

RIGHT
Walls on the landing switch to a blue hue for the bedroom levels.

OPPOSITE
Walls in 'Mischief' by Designers Guild give this central area a strong identity.

BELOW
Mintons went on to produce richly glazed designs, along with classic encaustic tiles. Mintons catalogue, 1870.

ENCAUSTIC FLOOR TILES

The Mintons ceramics factory, established in 1793, did much to popularize the age-old process of making encaustic tiles, where different colours of clay are set into sections of a mould and then fused to form a pattern during firing. In these inlaid designs, the pattern runs all the way through the tile, rather like a stick of seaside rock. Modern tile-makers have successfully revived this tradition, but with less fussy, clean-lined geometric shapes. Encaustic tiles are porous, and must be well sealed to protect them from discolouration, stains and damage.

A cheaper option is porcelain tiles, with the pattern painted or printed on top of the tile. They are not as durable as encaustic tiles, but work well as a less expensive way of tiling a large expanse of wall or floor.

TRADITIONAL

This selection of antique Victorian encaustic tiles from UK Architectural Heritage shows the variety of patterns that were available.

MODERN

'Azores',
 Fired Earth
'Lunatic',
 Maison Bahya
'Ondine',
 Maison Bahya

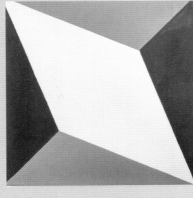

'Eventail',
 Mini Labo for
 Maison Bahya
'Vigo',
 Bert & May
'Luna',
 Bert & May

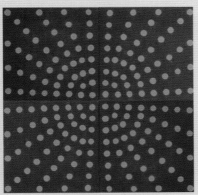

PRACTICALITY AND BEAUTY

This southwest London home opens into a relatively small entrance area, so to create more space, owner Chris Graves turned the room opposite the front door into a boot room, decorated in a luminous shade of green. It had previously been part of the next-door drawing room, but Chris, who runs the interior design studio Clarence & Graves, reinstated the original wall, reclaiming the space and restoring the proportions of the room.

Coats, bags and hats all have their own designated place, and there's also a built-in bench and a log store. The old door was replaced with a larger archway, which acts as a frame for the delicious colour combination of 'Arsenic' and 'Setting Plaster', both by Farrow & Ball – shades given extra zing by the chequerboard flooring. The unadorned window at the far end adds a sense of classical balance, and allows light to flow into the boot room – an unusual bonus.

BELOW LEFT
Tongue-and-groove panelling brings a rustic touch to this urban home.

BELOW
An archway instead of a door means more light and less architectural clutter.

OPPOSITE
A modern window is outlined in 'Arsenic' to match the panelling and skirting.

BELOW
Floor-to-ceiling cupboards add extra storage in designer Afroditi Krassa's home.

BELOW RIGHT
An under-stair cupboard is ideal for stashing away shoes and other bits and pieces.

OPPOSITE, TOP LEFT
A shallow cupboard fits into the gap where a doorway to the living room used to be.

OPPOSITE, TOP RIGHT
Nikos Koulouras's wall-hung bike racks make the most of every inch.

OPPOSITE, BOTTOM LEFT
A console table with space for shoes suits the style of Lisa Jewell's home.

OPPOSITE, BOTTOM RIGHT
Designer Sam Godsal fitted sliding panels to conceal shelves and a coat rack.

SLIMLINE STORAGE

Creating enough hallway storage – a necessity for modern family life – is an ongoing challenge in any home, and designers and homeowners have come up with ingenious ideas to make the most of these tricky spaces. If your hall is wide enough, one simple and elegant solution is to place a console table along one wall, with space for shoes underneath. For narrower entryways, a slim shelf will suffice for keys and letters, but bulkier items will need to be hidden away in under-stairs areas. Maximize these spaces by fitting a bespoke pull-out drawer or a selection of low-profile hooks. A slimline cupboard can even be set into the frame of a former doorway into another room room – as seen in this North London home designed by Emilie Fournet (opposite, top left).

VICTORIAN MEETS MID-CENTURY

Interior designer Mairead Turner is an unabashed fan of vintage style and colour. Her Victorian house on the Isle of Anglesey in northern Wales is an homage to retro style, which becomes abundantly clear as soon as you walk into the pattern-rich hallway. She used a bold wallpaper as her starting point, carrying the colours into her choice of paint: blue-green 'Pleats' on the woodwork and stairs and vivid 'Yellow Pink' below the dado rail, both by Little Greene. The wild card in this upbeat palette is 'Hellebore', a dusky pink shade on the ceiling.

BELOW LEFT
Rather than fitting a runner, Mairead painted the staircase to create a cohesive look.

BELOW
A black three-armed pendant light strikes a contemporary note.

OPPOSITE
The first-floor landing is used as a second workspace, with a 'peacock' chair and a faux stag head.

It is fitting that the key to the design – 'Hencroft' wallpaper from Little Greene's National Trust collection – has its roots in the late Victorian era. The stylized cowslips were inspired by a piece of embroidery created at the Leek Embroidery Society in Staffordshire, which was founded in 1879 by Elizabeth and Thomas Wardle, a collaborator of William Morris.

In this version, however, the colours are less staid and serious 1870s and more groovy 1970s. Mairead has worked the wallpaper into her own personal style, adding vintage prints – she and her husband love scouring markets, eBay and charity shops for finds – and lighting that adds a hint of modernity. Her decorative scheme is proof of how pattern can be used to create a bold, uplifting welcome in a hallway.

RIGHT
Vintage paintings are in keeping with the retro mood Mairead has created in her home.

OPPOSITE
The bright colours in the hallway give way to pinks and purples in the workroom.

LIVING ROOMS

Whether a morning room or a modest parlour, the living spaces of the Victorian home were where the best objects and furnishings would be on display, serving as an indicator of the residents' wealth, taste and class. Today, homeowners are free to let their personalities shine through in their choice of decor, from punchy colours and patterns to art and furniture. Layouts, too, are adaptable, with the ground-floor reception rooms often joined together to create a sense of flow.

ON P. 40
Gilt-edged glamour in Annabel White's Victorian home.

OPPOSITE
In Scarlett Gowing's house, delicate lights by Tom Dixon highlight the stained glass.

BELOW
Fireplaces and grates in a Horncastle & Son catalogue, 19th century.

A FORMAL GRANDEUR

KERBS,
ALL BRASS. ALL BLACK. BLACK AND BRASS.
BLACK AND STEEL. MARBLE.

FIRE BRASSES, FROM 11 6.
FIRE BRASS RESTS,
All Brass, from 5/-; Black and Brass, from 6/-;
Black and Steel, from 7 6.

"The Abbotsford" Tile Grate, Best Finish, with Tile Sides, from £3 3s.

ASHPANS, WITH BLACK, BRIGHT, OR BRASS FRONTS.

Special Designs for Tile Hearths on Application.

TILE REGISTER GRATES, from £1 10s.

The "Cambridge" Slow Combustion and Heat Economising Grate, with Tile Sides, from 40 -.

Well-off Victorians would have had a house with two or more living spaces, with each room having a clear function and none of the spilling over of activities into other areas seen in modern open-plan living. In a three-storey townhouse, guests would be ushered into the morning room on the ground floor, before progressing to the dining room on the floor above and then to a drawing room (the term derives from 'withdrawing'). In a middle-class semi, that journey would be truncated, with guests entertained in a ground-floor drawing room at the front.

Either way, a house's main social space was decorated in what was seen as a typically feminine style, with wallpapers and fabrics in light colours. In larger homes, this colour scheme would contrast with the library or billiards room, both considered to be the preserve of men and decorated accordingly in sombre colours with oak or mahogany bookcases, velvet curtains and marble fireplace surrounds. Turkish or Moorish influences might have also crept in, indulging the Victorian gentleman's view of himself as a man of the world with 'exotic' tastes.

Decorating was a serious business, and by the 1880s a new breed of writers was on hand to offer advice. One of the most prolific, Mrs J.E. Panton, the daughter of the artist William Powell Frith, devised rules for everything from how many curtains to hang at a window (up to four) to the best place to buy bamboo side tables (Liberty, naturally). Her books, along with the many illustrated catalogues produced by manufacturers, were aimed squarely at the emergent middle class. The implication was that the upper classes had the advantage of having inherent taste, while others needed a little more help.

By the 1880s, a new breed of writers was on hand to offer advice, along with the many illustrated catalogues produced by manufacturers.

With so much pressure to make the right choices, furnishing a home became a source of anxiety. In *Our Mutual Friend* (1865), Charles Dickens highlighted this insecurity with his descriptions of Mr and Mrs Veneering, a couple so keen to fit in and have the latest fashions that their furniture is still tacky with varnish.

This desire to make the right impression went hand-in-hand with decorating trends that relied on a sense of artifice. It was an era that celebrated fakery, with textured wallpapers such as Anaglypta and Lincrusta, faux woodgrain and marbling, and trompe-l'oeil friezes. It was common practice to stain floorboards black around the edges of a room but leave the centre untreated, where it would be covered by a rug. The same trick was sometimes repeated with parquet flooring, by laying expensive timber around the edges and cheaper floorboards in the middle.

Another quirk of Victorian life that has survived in our homes is the way that internal doors are hinged to aid privacy. Doors into living rooms were deliberately hung to open into the room, rather than against the wall. This allowed servants to knock, then slowly open a door, keeping themselves hidden from view for as long as possible and, if necessary, giving the occupants time to arrange themselves decorously.

ABOVE
Embossed flock wallpaper patterns from a William Woollams & Co. catalogue, 1881.

OPPOSITE
A modern reinterpretation of a wall tapestry in Suzanne Sharp's home.

OVERLEAF
Solange Azagury-Partridge mixes chintz with Moroccan textiles for an enveloping feel.

SOCIABLE SPACES

The trick is to celebrate a house's heritage while injecting a more relaxed, modern feel that reflects how we live now.

ABOVE
Internal glazing brings a modern touch to Sam Godsal's rear living room.

OPPOSITE
Punchy colours inject personality into this home designed for Danielle Bux.

One reason the Victorian house remains so enduringly popular is that despite the proliferation of rip-it-out-and-start-again decorators of the late 20th century, it is still relatively easy to find houses that have retained their original character. The trick is to celebrate a house's heritage while injecting a more relaxed, modern feel, adapting the interior so that it works for how we live now.

The living room, or rooms, is still a place where we socialize and entertain, but it is also a family space we use every day, rather than keeping for 'best'. The traditional configuration of the double ground-floor living space – with a reception room at the front and a dining room at the rear – demands careful consideration to prevent the back room from becoming redundant. In her scheme for a house in Notting Hill (p. 60), interior designer Flora Soames solves this conundrum by giving each space a clear identity, ensuring a continuity and sense of flow between the two rooms.

Homeowners Pandora Sykes (p. 50), Annie Sloan (p. 54) and Lucinda Chambers (p. 70) each demonstrate in their own houses the power of the right paint shade, along with highly individual ways of displaying art and vintage finds to add an extra dose of personality. When it comes to blending old and new architecture, Annabel White's home in Ladbroke Grove, West London, is a shining example (p. 104), and Jo Berryman's manor house in Somerset is a masterclass in reworking history with a creative eye (p. 72).

A VINTAGE TREASURE TROVE

In the living room of her semi-detached home in Kensal Rise, northwest London, writer and broadcaster Pandora Sykes has included a few subtle nods to the Victorians' fascination with all things Japanese, from a bamboo side table to the artwork on the walls. The derrière of a vase by Anissa Kermiche perched on an alcove shelf, however, along with the leopard-print curtains at the bay window, make it clear this is no den of faux-Victoriana.

The mustard shade of paint on the walls brings year-round warmth into the room, and contrasts brilliantly with the glossy fire-engine red used on the archway into the adjoining space – a reminder that this is an interior that soothes and invigorates in equal measure. Yes, there are dainty lampshades and bobbin side tables, but they sit alongside modern design surprises like an ultra-contemporary glass coffee table from Eichholtz.

There is a strong show of vintage finds, as Pandora is a champion of buying pre-loved, partly from a sustainability angle, but also because something spotted at an early morning market or online will always feel unique and outlive passing trends. Her reupholstered armchairs – a shapely 1940s number and a more refined mid-century design – both come with a whisper of the past, but now slide into a fresh 21st-century scheme, ready for a new lease of life.

OPPOSITE
Pandora's workspace lies to the left of the arch, outlined in glossy red.

ABOVE LEFT
A creative edit of fabrics stand out against walls painted in 'India Yellow' by Farrow & Ball.

LEFT
Bobbin detailing, a feature of 19th-century mass-produced furniture, is enjoying a revival.

THE GREAT COLLECTORS

The 19th-century fashion for displaying favourite objects in cabinets, under glass domes or on a mantelpiece was a large part of the decorative style of the time. The queen of household tips, Mrs J.E. Panton, even went so far as to claim that the display of 'our dearest treasures' in the parlour reflected the high moral standards that were maintained in the home. For the wealthy, such collections indicated a finely tuned sense of taste. With the rise of factory-made pottery, however, even modest homes could have a special ornament on display. Today, collections are more about individual taste than moral rectitude, blending groovy mid-century furniture with florid Victoriana or bold art with family photographs.

ABOVE
Mementoes and family photos mingle with artworks in Alex and Mishari Al-Bader's home.

RIGHT
Suzanne Sharp is an avid collector of modern furniture and contemporary artworks.

OPPOSITE
With her eye for colour, Suzanne brings together collectibles from different eras.

PLAYFUL COLOURS AND FASCINATING FINDS

In the Oxfordshire home of renowned paint and colour expert Annie Sloan, the two ground-floor reception rooms have been knocked through to make a double-space, with paint used to differentiate the two halves. The rear room is painted in 'Schinkel Green', and the front is in the more muted 'French Linen'; both are from Annie's own range of wall paints. Although quite different in mood, the jewel-green and grey-brown shades act as effective backdrops to her vast collection of art and curios.

In the livelier rear room, paintings and prints shine out against the lush walls and are a deliberate mix of old and new, with recognizable prints hung next to works by unknown artists. For Annie, this instinctive approach to hanging art is a way to subtly highlight the common threads and influences that have woven their way through works of art over the centuries.

Rich colours also come in the form of furniture, with a vintage sofa in just the right shade of ruby-red and a bright yellow side table. The walls behind the alcove shelves have also been painted in an interesting way, with sections in orange and a golden ochre – colours that appear on a larger scale in the front section of this living space, creating a colour link between the two halves.

OPPOSITE
Annie has filled her shelves with objects that have caught her eye and continue to inspire.

ABOVE RIGHT
A vintage embroidered sofa in ruby-red creates a strong contrast.

RIGHT
A slim side table painted by Annie adds to the energetic mix of colours.

In the front room, the brown shade of paint feels calmer and more classic, with a vivid strip of terracotta orange at the top of one wall adding a jolt of modernity – a reminder that this is a home founded on colour, playful combinations and fascinating finds. When she's in France, where she also has a home, Annie can't resist stopping off at brocantes and vide graniers (roadside attic sales), but her most precious belongings are those that conjure up memories of family and special places. Annie will doubtless continue to experiment with colour in this double-living space, but ultimately it is a place for personal treasures, making it a pleasure to spend time in.

OPPOSITE
The curtains are in Annie's 'Tacit' pattern; while the chandelier is 1960s French.

RIGHT
Annie deliberately blends antique with modern and delights in unexpected pairings.

BELOW
Jo Berryman chose 'Charlotte's Locks' by
Farrow & Ball to wake up this historic space.

PAINT SHADES

These days, we can pick and choose from a vast range of
colours, and any mistakes can be painted over easily. For
the Victorian homeowner, however, decorating was a longer-
term commitment. Paint wasn't sold in shops by the tin,
and each purchase was mixed to order and applied by a
professional decorator.

Strong reds and greens dominated in the 1850s and '60s,
partly because these rich colours were the perfect backdrop
for gilt picture frames and mirrors, and less likely to show
the smut generated by candles, open fires and gas lights. More
muted shades such as sage green, plum and rose gained favour
in the 1870s, with lighter creams and off-whites returning to
prominence in the Arts and Crafts schemes of the latter part
of the century. Window frames and doors were likely to be
painted dark brown or green, or given a woodgrain effect,
but pale paint on woodwork was a feature of some Queen
Anne Revival homes of the 1870s and '80s.

All of these fashions can be recreated by the higher-end
paint suppliers, who carry ranges of archive colours for an
authentic look. Combining these with the more vibrant
21st-century shades gives a unique Victorian Modern mix.

TRADITIONAL

'Dark Brunswick
Green',
Little Greene
'French Grey',
Little Greene
'Purple Brown',
Little Greene

'Bronze Red',
Little Greene
'Smalt',
Craig & Rose
'Light Gold',
Little Greene

MODERN

'Schinkel Green',
Annie Sloan
'Wimborne White',
Farrow & Ball
'Deep Reddish
Brown',
Farrow & Ball

'Rose',
Edward Bulmer
Natural Paint
'Laughton's Blue',
Adam Bray for
Papers and Paints
'HC52 Moorish
Yellow',
Papers and Paints

A SUBTLE USE OF TEXTURES

The grand proportions of this house on an iconic street in Notting Hill, West London, provided ample inspiration for interior designer Flora Soames, whose clients wanted a family home that would reflect their personalities, as well as tap into the building's character and historic past.

With the front and rear living spaces already exuding plenty of grandeur, Flora decided not to complicate things by adding too many patterns. Instead, she chose furniture shapes with gentle curves that complemented each other, including two glamorous Milo Baughman-designed swivel chairs, upholstered in a deep blue velvet with scalloped detailing and brass bases, placed alongside a modern B&B Italia sofa in a dusty pink linen. There's an easy flow between the two halves of the room, in part aided by the use of a hemp wallcovering from Phillip Jeffries. Its near-invisible texture helps to unify the spacs, as do the bespoke rugs from Vanderhurd.

BELOW
The front portion of the double-living space exudes a quiet luxury.

OPPOSITE
The sheen of the brass tables, mirrors and marble fireplace are undercut by the densely woven hemp wallcovering.

Works of art have been carefully chosen to suit the proportions of the room, and two Venetian mirrors on either side of the fireplace – a restrained marble design – create the suggestion of alcoves. The handsome windows at either end of the double-space are dressed simply with plain curtains, allowing the beauty of the Victorian architecture to speak for itself.

LEFT
Glazed double-doors are a gentle update to the Victorian door opening.

OPPOSITE
A serene spot at the back of the house, with 'Crillon' chairs from Soane Britain and a 1970s Lucite table by Lion in Frost.

GLAMOUR FROM SEVERAL DECADES

This handsome, double-fronted mid-Victorian villa in West London underwent a major renovation involving the relocation of a redesigned staircase and opening up the entire rear elevation of the house. It was important to owners Annabel and Jos White, however, as well as their architect Basil Walter of BWArchitects, that the two front rooms on either side of the central hallway retained their historic character – with a few judicious adjustments.

The doorways into both spaces from the hall were enlarged and fitted with sliding pocket doors, creating an easy flow of movement between the two rooms, the wide hallway and the back section of the house. One of the rooms (pictured on these pages) is used for social gatherings, while its opposite number across the way functions more as a family snug. Annabel asked her friend Suzanne Sharp (see also p. 28) to design the interiors, and the result is a luscious example of cherry-picking from different eras.

BELOW LEFT
The enlarged doorway opens into the central hall, which leads to the spacious kitchen-diner.

BELOW
Hollywood Recency touches shine out in a scheme that is both luxe and relaxed.

OPPOSITE
A writing desk in the bay window gives this sociable space an extra dimension.

The subtly updated fireplace with a black marble surround provides the focal point, its modernity tempered by the gilt 19th-century mirror that hangs above. In front of it, a 1970s coffee table and mirror-glass cube mix easily with glamorous brass bookcases from Soane Britain, themselves inspired by an 18th-century French étagère. The rug is by Suzanne for The Rug Company, while the palm-tree floor lamp from Maison Jansen adds unabashed glamour. This is a scheme that refuses to be pinned down to a single period – and is all the better for it.

OPPOSITE
Updated panelling around the walls retains a historic mood. The sofa is from Howe London.

RIGHT
A florid 19th-century mirror from Rose Uniacke hangs above the more restrained fireplace.

WINDOW TREATMENTS

The sash window is a key feature of Victorian architecture. In 1851, the abolition of window tax and excise duties on glass coincided with recent advances in glass-making. Previously, windows had been made by blowing and spinning discs of 'crown glass', which were then cut into smaller squares or rectangles. New methods allowed larger areas of molten glass to be poured onto a flat surface, allowing windows to have four panes, and two panes by the 1870s.

Operated via an internal system of weights and cords, the sash window was also extremely practical: in summer, the top and bottom sashes could be opened to allow for a flow of air. Windows acted as part of a house's ventilation system, as they do today, reducing damp and allowing the building to breathe.

Original windows can be reconditioned by fitting brushes into the frames and replacing the old glass with double- or triple-glazing. If the frames themselves need to be replaced, hardwood is an ideal, if expensive, option, but modern materials such as aluminium or uPVC can work if the proportions are in keeping with the architecture. Dressing windows – with thick curtains, blinds or shutters – is down to personal taste, but it's a bonus if the style enhances the beauty of an original or reconditioned window.

ABOVE
Reconditioned windows in a Victorian school only need simple grey roller blinds.

LEFT
Muslin panels and Roman blinds maximize sunlight in Sandra Barrio von Hurter's home.

OPPOSITE, TOP LEFT
Lucy Russell took an iridescent shade of blue into the window frame for wraparound impact.

OPPOSITE, TOP RIGHT
Simple roller blinds show off the shape of Chris Graves's bay windows.

OPPOSITE, BOTTOM LEFT
A window seat has been added beneath a clean-lined modern replacement window.

OPPOSITE, BOTTOM RIGHT
Practical shutters make a bold statement in this interior design by The Vawdrey House.

BELOW
Mid-century, rustic and contemporary ceramics are united by shape and colour.

BELOW RIGHT
Framed wallpaper samples add to the dynamic mix of stripes.

OPPOSITE
Walls painted in Little Greene's 'Firefly' provide a stunning backdrop to the rattan furniture and a rug made by Turkish weavers for Lucinda's company Colville.

COMFORT AND COLLECTIONS

For fashion director and designer Lucinda Chambers, style cannot exist without comfort. Her late Victorian townhouse in Shepherd's Bush, West London, is alive with colour, texture and interesting shapes, but the overall impression is one of a comfortable home that is full of memories. Even the choice of paint in the living room tells a family story: this space used to be the children's playroom, and the red and yellow shades were inspired by her youngest son's favourite Lego building blocks.

In both fashion and interiors, Lucinda is renowned for her interesting juxtapositions, placing objects or fabrics in new contexts so that their beauty can be seen with a fresh eye. In this room, mid-century shapes mingle with modern ceramics, blowsy florals mix with deckchair stripes, and rattan chairs sit alongside a traditional squishy sofa. It is an approach that would be anathema to the Victorian collector, but is true to the modern joy of decorating.

OPPOSITE
Beyond the formal arched doorway, furniture from different eras brings the house to life.

BELOW
The original shutters and cornicing are now partnered by a modern wallpaper pattern, 'Leo' by Pierre Frey.

OVERLEAF
Circular 1960s shapes, including a 'Ball' chair by Eero Aarnio, soften a once austere space.

THE FUTURISTIC MANOR HOUSE

In deference to the stately roots of her Somerset manor house, interior designer Jo Berryman refers to its double-living space as the 'parlour', but has updated the interior in her own inimitable style. The ceilings needed to be restored, but Jo liked the stripped-back effect so much that she decided not to paint them and leave them as they were.

The generous space, divided by an archway, is furnished with louche, 20th-century seating throughout, with a pair of 1960s Swedish sofas, upholstered in cobalt-blue velvet, in one half and futuristic examples by William Andrus in the other. In both sections, brass and opaline pendants by CTO Lighting work as modern chandeliers. For Jo, it is these juxtapositions that stir up creative tension and breathe life into an old home.

SIMPLE ARCHITECTURAL ELEGANCE

At first glance, the style of this pared-back, contemporary living space in Highgate, North London, might seem light years away from the house's Victorian roots, but the design choices have been closely informed by the original architecture. This double-fronted home is in a conservation area, and has been sensitively reimagined by architects Michaelis Boyd (see p. 24), drawing on the building's traditional focal points and satisfying symmetry.

The doorway into the living room, which lies to the right of the hallway, has been enlarged and fitted with steel-framed Crittall doors that let in ample light and echo the glazing running along the wall of the rear reception room. The family loves entertaining, and the uncluttered space is ideal for larger gatherings, with the main seating area arranged beneath the window. New wall panelling extends around the entire space, complementing the existing historic shutters – a subtle visual detail that pays homage to the past without dipping into pastiche.

BELOW LEFT
New panelling maintains a subtle link with the past.

BELOW
In the rear half of the space, glazing links the room to adjoining areas.

OPPOSITE
Classic 20th-century furniture and lighting designs sit comfortably within the Victorian frame.

The interior design by Simone McEwan of Nice Projects makes use of the best of contemporary furniture shapes. The angles of twin 'Utrecht' armchairs by Gerrit Rietveld for Cassina are balanced out by the smooth curves of a coffee table by Malgorzata Bany and the less structured shape of the 'Ghost' sofa beneath the window, designed by Paola Navone for Gervasoni. Sculptural floor lamps by Isamu Noguchi and a classic pendant light by George Nelson for Herman Miller complete the perfect geometry of shapes, which have plenty of space to breathe within this light, bright update of Victorian architecture.

LEFT
Beyond the door is the entertainment room, keeping the living room screen-free.

OPPOSITE
Tall Crittall doors form a crisp, beautiful entrance to the room.

DINING ROOMS

Decorum reigned in the Victorian dining room, which would be decorated in rich colours and lined with family portraits. In the contemporary version, this space can still conjure up a sense of occasion, but with far less formality. Now, it is more common for the eating area to work in conjunction with other rooms of the house, such as an adjoining living space or as part of an open-plan kitchen. Large or small, these spaces offer plenty of scope to bring together the best of old and new.

ON P. 80
A side-return extension gave Hannah Wright and George Sims their dining area, which they clad in cedar.

OPPOSITE
Mid-century furniture and a contemporary light bring a fresh feel to this space in Scarlett Gowing's home.

BELOW
Fish dishes from a new edition of *Mrs Beeton's Every Day Cookery and Housekeeping*, 1890.

A SENSE OF OCCASION

With affluent Victorians enjoying meals that could last up to nine courses, the dining room was where guests would have had plenty of time to sit and admire their host's taste, and the decor needed to impress accordingly. At the time, the dining room was often the first space to be decorated, in a style that tended towards darker, richer and what were seen as more 'masculine' colours. Shades such as claret and deep green were also practical, as they hid the sooty residue left by gas lights, candles and open fires. The intricate patterns of plaster ceiling roses were also both decorative and functional, catching the worst of the soot; some designs even included flues to direct the smoke outside.

Traditionally, the dining room would have an austere and imposing black fireplace, balanced by a lighter version in white marble in the drawing room. A mahogany dining table, upholstered chairs and a sideboard displaying the best china were standard; on the floor, a rug might have been topped by a drugget, a simple woven cloth for catching crumbs or spills. A dado rail would have run around the room to protect expensive wallpaper from scuffs when chairs were pushed back against the wall. Naturally, the pattern-loving Victorians took the opportunity to use the dado rail as a visual divider, with different decoration above and below, while the rail itself might also be painted with small decorative motifs.

Every part of the Victorian dining experience was carefully considered, from the ornaments that graced the table and mantelpiece to the dishes that were served. Isabella Beeton is associated with cookery today, but her books and magazine columns also included plenty of advice on how the mistress of the house should conduct herself and maintain a harmonious home. The rise of such manuals was a sign that society was in flux. The middle-class wife – not to mention her servants – were all slotting into a changing urban world, where information was being handed down by an outside expert in the form of a book or newspaper article rather than from mother to daughter.

Of course, in the Victorian home the hard work that went on in the kitchen remained hidden behind closed doors, and the layouts of our inherited 19th-century houses attest to this. But today we prefer our dining rooms to be connected to the kitchen, rather than separated from it. Cooking has become a social activity as well as a necessity, making the kitchen-diner the hub of family life.

The rear kitchen-diner extension is a common feature of many updated urban Victorian homes, often with rooflights and glass doors opening onto the garden. When sensitively done, extending into the side return or back garden can create extra space that works harmoniously with the proportions of the original layout. If you're planning an extension with lots of glazing, a solar-control coating on the glass will prevent it from getting uncomfortably hot in summer; in colder months, double- or triple-glazing will reduce heat waste. Acoustic layers can also be laminated between panes of toughened glass to provide sound insulation – useful in busy city locations.

Along with recipes, Mrs Beeton gave advice on how the mistress of the house should conduct herself and maintain a harmonious home.

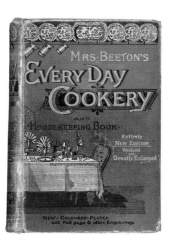

A MULTIPURPOSE SPACE

The modern dining room is well used by all the family, and easily doubles as a place for homework or hobbies, as well as for eating.

ABOVE
Nikos Koulouras's dining area sits at the centre of an open-plan space, between the kitchen and living room.

OPPOSITE
Freeform foliage and abstract art add colour to Steph Wilson's open-plan dining area in a converted school.

What unites the diverse Victorian Modern dining spaces shown on the following pages is flexibility. A place for eating might be part of an entirely open-plan studio, as in photographer Steph Wilson's former Victorian schoolhouse (opposite), but even when it is a separate room – as in Jo Berryman's manor house (p. 88) or Susannah Parker's former rectory (p. 90) – the modern dining room is well used by all the family, and easily doubles as a place for homework or hobbies, as well as for meals.

Whether created by knocking through two rooms or adding a rear extension, the open-plan kitchen-diner also has implications for kitchen design generally. It will need ample storage and preparation areas, as well as an extractor fan to take care of lingering smells, so that when you and your guests sit down to eat, you won't feel crowded out by cooking mess.

The table is the centrepiece of the dining area, and an opportunity to show off your individual taste and style. But it also needs to be the right size: generous enough to seat everyone, but not so large that it overwhelms the room. A petite table is a practical choice in a small room, or to create a secondary eating space. In Annabel White's home (p. 106), a classic 'Tulip' table provides a cool, calm centrepiece in the lower ground-floor games and TV room. With a view out onto the garden, it provides the ideal spot for enjoying morning coffee or evening cocktails.

REVEALING LAYERS
OF HISTORY

For interior designer Jo Berryman, renovating her Somerset manor house was about blending the past with the present. Rather than giving the walls a too-perfect look, she decided to leave a raw-plaster finish, with patches peeping out from underneath to reveal the house's previous layers. The pale-pink walls also balance out the room's dark wooden doors and brown marble fireplace.

The chandelier is another deft blend of old and new, adorned with glittery black chains instead of crystals and candle cups. The table and chairs also have a more modern feel, with orange leather that links with the paint shade in the adjoining room (see p. 58). Contemporary shelving and prints are the final ingredients in a design that acknowledges how Jo is one in a long line of owners who have gently adapted the house's character to suit her own taste.

OPPOSITE
Hefty stained-glass doors open onto a room that deftly blends past and present.

BELOW LEFT
Shell sconces from Soane Britain shine out against plaster-pink walls.

BELOW
Original alcoves are filled with 20th-century memorabilia.

CREATING AN ATMOSPHERE

Interior designer Susannah Parker's dining room in a former rectory in Devon comes into its own in the evening, when the candles are lit and the reflective surfaces catch the light to create a magical atmosphere. Her masterstroke was to fit antique mirrored glass into three sections of panelling – painted in Farrow & Ball's 'Mole's Breath', which takes on a mellow lilac tone in certain light – with a further piece above the marble fireplace. The glass reflects the glow from holophane lanterns based on old Parisian street lamps.

The proportions of the furniture are also important, with the long antique table complementing the mid-century Ercol dining chairs surprisingly well. Accessories, too, have been carefully thought through, with plenty of shine and gleam coming from the collections of glassware, ceramics, brass candlestick holders and small glass medicine bottles. The original shutters have been painted in the same shade as the walls for a seamless continuity.

BELOW LEFT
The vintage bamboo side table and upholstered chair were junk-shop finds.

BELOW
Antique brass candlesticks mingle with smoky-toned modern glassware.

OPPOSITE
The addition of mirrored glass helps this space feel magical in candlelight.

THE RIGHT DINING CHAIR

The choice of dining chair comes down to style and comfort. It also needs to work in tandem with the table, so a chair with a gently curved back will work well with a circular table or soften the blocky feel of a rectangular one. A farmhouse table can be partnered with similarly rustic chairs, but when buying vintage chairs, always try them out first, as the people they were originally designed for were considerably shorter.

Dining chairs need to fit easily beneath the table; if they are carvers, the arms should be set low enough to make this possible, or gently tapered so that most of the chair can fit underneath. Like an office chair, a dining chair should envelop you: if you find yourself slumping or wishing for a cushion for the small of your back, it's probably the wrong shape. A built-in banquette seat is always a smart space-saving option in a corner.

BELOW LEFT
Louise Carlisle's kitchen from Plain English has a built-in banquette in red leather.

BELOW
Carver chairs by Berdoulat with the designers' profiles cut into the back splats.

OPPOSITE, TOP LEFT
Blue velvet upholstery echoes the window seat and stained glass in Lisa Jewell's home.

OPPOSITE, TOP RIGHT
'Wishbone' chairs by Hans J. Wegner in a house designed by Michaelis Boyd.

OPPOSITE, BOTTOM LEFT
French-inspired chairs and Sanderson archive wallpaper suit Louise Carlisle's dining room.

OPPOSITE, BOTTOM RIGHT
Warm-toned mid-century chairs work with the pink walls in Sam Godsal's kitchen-diner.

IN KEEPING WITH ITS CHARACTER

In her interior design for a house in East London, Emilie Fournet used rich colours and vintage furniture to celebrate the building's original character, while adding some modern twists. Although the house dates from the early Victorian period, inspiration came from the creaky, cosy spaces of the 18th-century silkweavers' houses in nearby Spitalfields.

The original doors between the breakfast room at the front and the redesigned kitchen at the rear were rehung as sliding pocket doors to take up less space. On the walls is an archive colour from Farrow & Ball, which – along with the red of the armchair fabric and vintage rug – brings energy into the space. The panelling and shelving have also been painted in the same shade, and the floorboards given a dark stain to foster a historic atmosphere.

COMPACT SPACES

Dining isn't always a grand affair and in a tight space, a round table or a vintage style can work well. In Ana Perez's converted outbuilding in Norfolk, chairs from an old chapel suit the size of the small farmhouse table, and a pew fits neatly into the corner with space for storage boxes underneath. In Wimbledon, Lisa Mehydene has her morning coffee at a second, smaller dining table, pairing it with mid-century chairs that are unobtrusive yet stylish. Robert Storey also opted for vintage chairs in his home, but his table is a far punchier number, with vibrant splashes of colour. At a push, two more chairs could be added for lunch with friends or a cosy supper for four.

ABOVE LEFT
In Ana Perez's home, a chapel pew and chairs look at home around a farmhouse table.

ABOVE
Lisa Mehydene opted for a high-low mix of chairs by Kai Kristiansen and an Ikea table.

OPPOSITE
Robert Storey pairs vintage 'Heart' chairs by Hans J. Wegner with a modern table designed by Dirk Van der Kooij.

A LIGHT AND AIRY FORMER PUB

The living spaces of this Victorian building have always been on the first floor, as it was the local pub until the 1970s. Mary Mulryan turned the old public bar and saloon into bedrooms, and kept the first floor as living spaces, including this kitchen-diner. Breaking with the pub's gloomy past, her aim was to bring in plenty of natural light and create a far more open, natural feel for the space.

The room was stripped back to the original brickwork, which was then lightened with coats of paint rather than concealed with plasterboard. The rafters and beams were also left uncovered and reconditioned instead. Mary chose a creamy grey shade of paint ('Drop Cloth' by Farrow & Ball), which complements the woven wicker furniture, seagrass flooring and the sawn-edged finish of the kitchen units. New steel-framed doors open onto a terrace that functions as an extra space, especially in summer.

BELOW
Sawn-edged cabinetry, beams and painted brick add to the modern rustic feel.

OPPOSITE
Glazed doors open onto a roof terrace that can be brought into use as an extra room.

OPPOSITE
Café chairs from Sunbury Antiques Market liven up a traditional table.

BELOW
Walls in sunny yellow act as a warm counterbalance to the metallic finishes.

BELOW RIGHT
Different colours of paint were used to pep up the existing kitchen cabinets.

A COLOURFUL TRANSFORMATION

This extended kitchen-diner is a welcoming, easygoing space that has been transformed by colour without any drastic changes or a huge outlay. A side-return extension had already been completed when jewelry designer Sandra Barrio von Hurter bought the house, but she saw scope to widen the run of glazing at the rear, adding two extra sections of glass to make the space feel closer to the garden and bring in extra light.

Then came the colours. Sandra wanted to add hot, vibrant hues throughout, using paint, fabrics and patterns. She had blinds made in Mulberry's 'Sailboat' linen and kept the candy-stripe colours in mind for the rest of the room. The walls in 'Orangery' by Farrow & Ball give a year-round dose of sunshine, while four woven pendants by Matilda Goad for edit58 add to the frivolous, fun atmosphere.

BELOW
A delicate chandelier suits the monochrome beauty of Leanne von Arx's Bath home.

BELOW RIGHT
Two sets of double-pendants cover all bases in Joe Barton's home by Field Day Studio.

OPPOSITE, TOP LEFT
Pastel-toned glass orbs reflect the vintage style of Leanne Chandler's barn conversion.

OPPOSITE, TOP RIGHT
Lucy Russell's super-sized dining table calls for equally generous lighting.

OPPOSITE, BELOW LEFT
Beech cupolas by Tamasine Osher provide a diffused glow in Kate Arbuthnott's design.

OPPOSITE, BELOW RIGHT
A single rattan shade forms a simple centrepiece in Chris Graves's dining room.

PENDANT LIGHTING

Whether you opt for a trio of modern pendants or a throwback to Victorian gas lights in the form of an antique chandelier, the received wisdom is that your chosen light should hang around 1 m (3 ft) above the dining table. This will give a fairly low, focused glow; a pendant that needs to illuminate an entire room will need to be hung much higher.

This is very much a flexible rule of thumb, however, and if your room has a low ceiling or your light is exceptionally large or elaborate, it is wise to sit at the table and check that the diners' faces won't be obscured. A dimmer switch is essential for creating the right atmosphere.

FRESH ARCHITECTURAL UNITY

The back half of Annabel and Jos White's mid-Victorian villa was reconfigured to create one large space, comprising the dining room, a seating area and the kitchen. The mood is almost tropical, with cane chairs and walls painted in a custom shade of pink and covered in delicate handpainted leaves by artist Timna Woollard. An 18th-century dresser stands against a wall of mirror glass, which reflects the kitchen at the other end of the room.

Architect Basil Walter of BWArchitects replaced the old staircase with a new sculptural structure, which resembles a gently unfurling ribbon. It leads up to bedrooms and down to the lower ground floor, which has a games room and a wall of glazing that opens onto the family's garden (overleaf).

ABOVE
Surrounded by palm fronds, rattan chairs by Viggo Boesen invite pre–dinner lounging.

LEFT
A serpentine chandelier from Ochre illuminates the table and Rupert Bevan-designed chairs.

OPPOSITE
The house's new staircase is more like a sculptural installation.

OVERLEAF
The punchy colours of the games room add drama to 'Selene' chairs by Vico Magistretti and a 'Tulip' table by Eero Saarinen.

KITCHENS

In grander houses, the kitchen was a hot and busy place, located as far as possible from the rest of the house. Today, it has evolved into a role that could not be more different: a sociable hub where family and friends gather together and meals are shared. Whether in a country home or an extended terraced house in the city, the kitchen has to be both practical and hardworking – but there is also plenty of scope to get creative with innovative design ideas.

ON P. 108
In Michaelis Boyd's design for a home in North London, the kitchen flows into the dining area.

OPPOSITE
Solange Azagury-Partridge's country kitchen blends tradition with a modern palette.

BELOW
As the century progressed, cast-iron cookers became ever more efficient and elaborate. J.L. Mott Iron Works catalogue, 1871.

LIFE BELOW STAIRS

In historic houses now open to the public, the old kitchen, scullery and butler's pantry tend to be where visitors linger, taking in the rows of shiny copper pots, the neatly organized silver, the cast-iron range cooker and the scrubbed surfaces for chopping vegetables and rolling pastry. Part of this fascination lies in the fact that a well-preserved kitchen gives an authentic glimpse into how life was lived in another century, with the same tasks that we do every day – apart from polishing the silver – carried out in an entirely different setting.

For the Victorians, the kitchen was a place of undisguised hard work. It was this labour – whether by the wife, a housekeeper or numerous staff in a grand house – which underpinned the smooth running of the household. In the 19th century, the kitchen was consigned to the basement or the rear of the house; in some homes, it might even have been in a separate building altogether. The aim was to keep the smells and constant clatter at a remove from the more genteel spaces, with servants often summoned by a bell.

Decor was determined by function, with tiled walls and wooden duck boards underfoot. Tongue-and-groove boarding was an alternative wallcovering, painted in gloss paint for a hygienic, washable surface. Sinks were not common in kitchens until the early 1900s, and washing up took place in a separate scullery, along with preparing meat and fish, scrubbing vegetables and doing the laundry.

In a smaller two-up, two-down working-class home, meals would be cooked on a stove in the back parlour, the warmest and most comfortable room of the house (even in small houses, a front room was left for 'best'). Cooking was far from elaborate, and restricted to making toast or warming up takeaway pies. For anything more involved, food would be taken to a local bakery and customers charged for each item that needed cooking. Terraced houses that backed onto a shared courtyard might have a communal scullery block and separate privy. On wash days, this was where neighbouring households did the laborious tasks associated with laundry, with water heated in the shared 'copper', a large metal vessel encased in brick or stone, and heated by a fire beneath it.

For the Victorians, keeping food fresh was an ongoing issue. Larger houses might have an icebox, with slabs of ice delivered by door-to-door sellers, but smaller houses made do with a larder or pantry, a walk-in cupboard with stone floors, shelves of slate or marble for keeping dairy items cool and hooks for hanging meat, and often a small window covered with a metal grille for ventilation.

Today, even with the excess of high-tech gadgets we have at our disposal, old-fashioned copper pans and antique chopping boards have become coveted and collectible items (see p. 122), and the old-fashioned larder is making a comeback in contemporary kitchen designs (see p. 138).

BELOW
Victorian coal scuttles kept fires and cooking ranges topped up in style. J.L. Mott Iron Works catalogue, 1882.

OPPOSITE
Modern everyday appliances in Leanne von Arx's gleaming kitchen.

For the Victorian home, the kitchen was a place of undisguised hard work. It was this labour that underpinned the smooth running of the household.

THE HEART OF THE HOME

Ensure that kitchen extensions feel connected to the rest of the home by using similar colours, motifs and materials.

ABOVE
A seamless design language in the linked kitchen-diner of Suzanne Sharp's home.

OPPOSITE
Susannah Parker updated the existing cabinets with a coat of 'Jack Black' paint by Little Greene.

Victorian terraces and semis often come with a narrow galley space at the back of the house, which would have been used as the scullery and/or kitchen. The most common way to expand this kitchen area is by extending into the side return; another option is to build an extension across the back of the house, ensuring that it feels connected to the rest of the home by using similar colours, motifs and materials.

This is exactly what Field Day Studio did in their redesign of Joe Barton's home in Brighton (p. 134), where the open-plan kitchen is characterized by a single, strong colour (warm yellow), set against glossy white tiles and steel-framed glazing – a combination repeated in the family bathroom upstairs, but with a burnt-orange shade on the bath (see p. 208). Designers Chris Graves (p. 124) and The Vawdrey House (p. 130) also harnessed the power of colour – dipping into varying shades of green – and have approached structural changes in different yet still sympathetic ways.

As a twist on the extension trend, architect Siri Zanelli expanded her kitchen, but stuck to the old L-shape layout with compelling results (p. 146). For Patrick Williams, it was a matter of starting from scratch; the beautiful kitchen he created in a former grocer's shop in Bath, however, looks anything but brand new (p. 116). And in her 19th-century Kentish barn (p. 140), Leanne Chandler also remains true to her home's roots by using rough and reclaimed textures.

MINING THE PAST
FOR INSPIRATION

Before beginning work on his mews house in Bath, Patrick Williams researched its history from the inside out. He discovered how the building began life in 1800 as a rough-and-ready pub called The Rising Sun, where Bath's sedan-chair carriers would take refreshment, and that by the end of the 19th century it formed part of a grocer's shop, selling wine and spirits.

When Patrick and his wife Neri, who together founded design studio Berdoulat, took the building on, along with a larger Georgian property that backs onto it, they focused on its time as a shop. A huge sash window was installed at the front – necessitating a chain system rather than weights, to take the 120 kg (265 lbs) load – and the old shop counter was reinstated in the same position shown on the 1890 plans, now marking the divide between the kitchen and a living area at the front.

BELOW LEFT
An antique cupboard with arched doors functions as a larder.

BELOW
Utilitarian clay sinks were bought from a Norfolk reclamation yard. The plate rack is a Berdoulat design.

OPPOSITE
Patrick and Neri live in a Georgian home that backs onto this Victorian building, linked by a covered courtyard.

Walking into this house feels like travelling back in time, with some important concessions made to modern living. Pieces that evoke a period feel include the dining table, reclaimed Victorian ceramic sinks and an antique cabinet that doubles as a larder. The plate rack, dining chairs and ceramic platters, however, are part of Berdoulat's own range of contemporary craft collaborations, which took inspiration from designs from the 18th and 19th centuries. The result is a home that draws on the artisanal traditions of the past, but builds on them to create a home that is considered and inspiring.

OPPOSITE
Plates by Lydia Hardwick for Berdoulat draw on 19th-century Burleigh Pottery designs.

RIGHT
The appliances and rise-and-fall pendant lights have an understated character.

OVERLEAF
The building's original shop counter has been reinstated in its rightful place.

POTS, PANS AND KITCHENALIA

Today we have air-fryers, stand mixers, food processors, taps that produce boiling water on demand, and more gadgets than we know what to do with. But the Victorian kitchen also had its fair share of time-savers, although they still required plenty of elbow grease to operate them, from hand-operated meat mincers to mechanical apple peelers and a device that ground up coffee beans. Antique kitchenalia is now highly collectible, and many items found in vintage shops or reclamation yards will still do an excellent job, including scales and chopping boards. Copper pans, a staple of the grand Victorian kitchen, are still prized for their beauty, as well as their heat-conducting properties, and add an authentic touch so the kitchen still feels like a hardworking, lived-in space.

BELOW LEFT
A hanging rail is a nod to the past in a former Bermondsey tannery by Howark Design.

BELOW
An array of vintage finds in Sarah Brown's home.

OPPOSITE
In the family kitchen at Deans Court, old copper pots and pans live on as a display.

THE TRANSFORMATIVE POWER OF GREEN

It took Chris Graves a while to settle on exactly the right shade of green for the Crittall doors in his kitchen, located on the garden level of a London townhouse. Rather than extend, he decided to make the best possible use of the existing footprint, replacing twin sash windows with glazing to transform the space and add light – as well as that luminous, uplifting shade of green.

The hob is integrated into the island (the chimney recess would have been another option), so that whoever is cooking can be part of the conversation, rather than having their back to the room. Chris and his partner Jolene describe the palette as reminiscent of a Wes Anderson film, and the retro green and pale-pink walls certainly add character. They lift the DeVol cabinets, in a classic darker green, while the floor tiles and wicker lampshades bring in the feel of sunlit Mediterranean spaces.

The natural, free-flowing striations of the marble splashback and worktop also breathe life into the scheme, and vintage finds – a cute chair and a desk in another delicious shade of green – make the entire space feel lived in and loved. White goods and pantry storage are tucked into a utility space adjoining the main kitchen, allowing items on the open shelving to err on the side of decorative.

ABOVE LEFT
A walk-in pantry area next to the main kitchen also houses larger appliances.

LEFT
Chris based his colour choice for the Crittall window frames on a coin-sized metal sample – a gamble that paid off.

OPPOSITE
Cabinets have traditional detailing, but the interior scheme as a whole feels fresh.

OVERLEAF
The green doors open onto a sunny terrace, created by excavating part of the garden.

BELFAST OR BUTLER'S SINK?

The two ceramic sinks we associate with the Victorian era have one simple difference: the Belfast sink was deeper, with an overflow weir on one side. This was because water was plentiful in Ireland, so that sinks could be filled to the top, allowing any excess to flow down the weir. The design was also more efficient at draining water away, as the overflow prevented pockets of air from creating a block. The butler's sink was the London version, shallower and without an overflow as the city's water supply was less reliable and sometimes scarce. Today, either design is a handsome addition to any kitchen, rustic or modern.

BELOW
A crisp white-on-blue design scheme by White Arrow in an 1850s farmhouse kitchen.

OPPOSITE, TOP LEFT
Decorative tiles make a vibrant splashback in Solange Azagury-Partridge's kitchen.

OPPOSITE, TOP RIGHT
A double Victorian-style sink in an interior scheme by Field Day Studio.

OPPOSITE, BOTTOM LEFT
Tiles from Bert & May bring geometric joy to Susannah Parker's kitchen.

OPPOSITE, BOTTOM RIGHT
Bare brick and a simple upstand partner the sink in Nikki Kellie's monochrome kitchen.

OPPOSITE
A mosaic floor with a black trim is integral
to the design.

BELOW
There is a clear sightline into the relaxed
seating area at the back of the house.

BELOW RIGHT
The opening between the living room and
the kitchen follows the angle of the rooflight.

A STREAMLINED HUB
TO A HOME

This home in northwest London, with interior design provided by The Vawdrey House, was extended to the rear and side. The kitchen sits at the centre of the ground-floor plan, illuminated by a run of rooflights on one side and steel-framed doors on the other, which open onto a still spacious side-return area, looping round to the garden behind the house.

The style is inspired by the owners' favourite eateries from around the globe, including the booths in New York City diners and the mosaic floors of Parisian cafés. A dash of London urban style comes in the form of a stainless-steel panel running along one side of the space. For every hard-edged, cool design feature, however, there is a softer one to keep things feeling balanced.

The L-shaped island wrapping around a leather breakfast nook is in warm-toned oak, and incorporates plenty of storage underneath. The 'wall of steel' hides away yet more storage, and at one end a door opens onto a utility room and pantry. The bold paint shade for the base units also keeps the space feeling modern and vibrant: imagine how different this space would feel with dark cabinetry as a partner to the slick steel ...

As the kitchen occupies a central position, doorways into the front living room and garden room to the rear allow the flow of light and air, with the openings showing a clear, easy progression through the house. The Victorian spaces have been preserved, with a gentle sense of movement introduced to allow the house to feel open, welcoming and ever-evolving.

RIGHT
A reclaimed cast-iron balcony is a historic touch, next to modern stainless-steel units.

OPPOSITE
Banquette seating is set around a marble table on salvaged metal legs.

BELOW
Freestanding wooden furniture supplements the yellow cabinetry.

BELOW RIGHT
An internal window lets plenty of light into the utility room, previously the kitchen.

OPPOSITE
The yellow paint shade is bespoke, working with crisp white tiles and vintage lights.

OVERLEAF
Modern glazing runs across the back of the house, with a dining area on the right.

MELLOW MEETS INDUSTRIAL

The kitchen in the Brighton home of screenwriter Joe Barton was previously located in the middle of the house, with a conservatory and family room at the rear. Interior designers Field Day Studio relocated it to the back, extending and joining up the other rooms to create one large, open kitchen-diner, with a breakout seating area centred around a wood-burning stove.

The old kitchen is now a chic utility room, glimpsed through an internal window fitted with steel-framed glazing. The same style of glazing runs across the entire back wall of the room and is repeated in the family bathroom. With its hefty exposed beams, stainless-steel island and utilitarian tiles, the new space is strong on industrial style, an effect that is tempered by the choice of paint for the units, gentle wood textures and plenty of leafy foliage.

ABOVE
Floating shelves are used to store everyday tableware in Mary Mulryan's former pub.

OPPOSITE, TOP LEFT
A mirror-backed cabinet is stacked with glassware designs by Christian Haas.

OPPOSITE, TOP RIGHT
The interior design by Emilie Fournet integrates shelves into the central island.

OPPOSITE, BOTTOM LEFT
A modern walk-in pantry by White Arrow.

OPPOSITE, BOTTOM RIGHT
A modern take on the kitchen dresser provides storage for crockery in Alex and Mishari Al-Bader's home.

STORAGE SOLUTIONS

Today, the walk-in pantry and larder are enjoying a revival, and feature in many contemporary built-in kitchens. These new and improved versions can be customized to suit taste and need, with shelving set into the doors, or a small worktop fitted to hide away the toaster, microwave and coffee machine. The traditional arrangement of open shelving ensures that items that are in constant use are to hand. But this doesn't mean that everything on the kitchen shelves is functional: works of art and decorative ceramics add life and colour when displayed alongside plates, mugs and glasses. Freestanding glass-fronted cabinets are always a good way to store tableware, and kitchen islands can be built with recessed shelves for displaying prettier items.

KENTISH HOPS AND GLOBAL FINDS

You could be forgiven for expecting the style of this kitchen in a 19th-century barn in Sissinghurst, Kent, to be 100 per cent rustic. Yes, there are Kentish hops hung from the rafters, but there are also bar stools that the owner spotted in Byron Bay, Australia, a pair of chandeliers that were woven in Bali, and salvaged doors from India. Leanne Chandler and her husband Luke wanted the kitchen to express the places the family have visited and where they live now, and sticking to a simple palette of monochromes, blended with plenty of natural textures, has helped them achieve this.

RIGHT
The front door of the house opens straight into this characterful kitchen.

OPPOSITE
Beyond is the dining room, which is also filled with rustic finds.

The concrete floor of the barn was rough and cracked, so the couple fitted parquet flooring that is a close match to the exposed beams and roofing timbers above. A central island includes a prep area, a second sink and plenty of storage, with drawers and handles that have the character of library cabinets to keep the look from being too 'kitcheny'.

The scheme works with the myriad vintage pieces that Leanne and Luke have picked up over the years, from the French confit pots that add a blast of mustard yellow to a mirror that doubles as a splashback above the sink. On shelves and hung from wall racks, carved wooden spoons and chopping boards make interesting displays when not in use. The brick walls are painted off-white, but Leanne asked a professional signwriter to paint the family's name above the doorway into their dining room, knowing this kitchen would be the heart of their home.

BELOW LEFT
Henry the cat has commandeered a little-used corner sink for a nap.

BELOW
A mirror in a vintage window frame creates an original splashback.

OPPOSITE
Beneath a vintage peg rail, reclaimed doors from India lead into the living room.

THE RECLAIMED KITCHEN

Vintage cabinets, farmhouse tables or worktops salvaged from school science labs can work wonders for bringing character into a kitchen. Reconditioned kitchen sinks can be found in salvage yards, and shop counters, former library display cases or freestanding cabinets from vintage fairs can also be pressed into service. As well as looking wonderful and cutting down on landfill, these secondhand treasures often cost far less than cupboards made in overseas factories and then shipped halfway around the globe.

BELOW LEFT
A long French farmhouse table is used as a kitchen island in Emily Huc's home.

BELOW
Salvaged timber was used for the cladding, as well as the cabinets and shelves, in a former farm outbuilding belonging to Ana Perez.

OPPOSITE
Lisa Valencia turned a workbench from a Spitfire factory into an unusual kitchen island.

OPPOSITE
The kitchen extension is a well-used seating area, with a chair from the Varier x Ingrid Bredholt collection.

BELOW
Large-format terrazzo tiles are used on the floor and steps up to the hallway.

BELOW RIGHT
The handleless cabinets in elm are simple and unobtrusive.

A MODEST EXTENSION

Architect Siri Zanelli's Victorian terrace is in a conservation area, and it was always her intention that the kitchen extension would remain subservient to the building. It adds 19 m² (204½ sq ft) – enough space to make a difference – but sticks to the original L-shaped floorplan, with a snug extending into the garden. Bare bricks echo the 19th-century brickwork at the front of the house, giving a sense of unity and cohesion.

Siri saved money by getting a local joiner to build the kitchen, using elm veneer on the cabinets and Douglas Fir cladding on the ceiling – which helps with the acoustics as the floor is tiled. A recessed 'box' for the sink area adds visual interest, breaking up what would have been a flat run of cabinets. This box motif is reversed in the snug, where the protruding window frame provides an extra surface for houseplants.

BEDROOMS

While the upper-class Victorian bedroom followed fashions in furniture, fabrics and wallpaper, ultimately it was a space that remained hidden from view. For women, it often doubled as a sitting room, which made it feel all the more personal and valued. The bedroom remains a restful retreat, but today's homeowners have found creative ways to reconfigure layouts or carve out new spaces in loft extensions. Children's bedrooms, too, offer myriad possibilities to decorate imaginatively.

THE RETREAT

ON P. 148
A minimalist version of the four-poster in Lisa Mehydene's bedroom.

OPPOSITE
In Pandora Sykes's home, the mouldings on the walls and the 'Lasso' print by Pierre Frey on the headboard create a cosseting space.

BELOW
Advertisement for a brass bedstead from Maple & Co, published in the *Illustrated London News*, 13 February 1892.

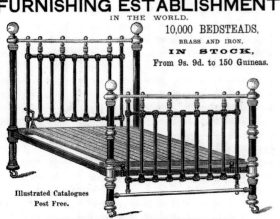

MAPLE & CO
LIMITED,
Tottenham Court Road, London, W,
THE LARGEST AND MOST CONVENIENT
FURNISHING ESTABLISHMENT
IN THE WORLD.
10,000 BEDSTEADS,
BRASS AND IRON,
IN STOCK,
From 9s. 9d. to 150 Guineas.

Illustrated Catalogues
Post Free.

"PATENT WOVEN WIRE MATTRESS."
The above BLACK and BRASS BEDSTEAD, with the PATENT WIRE WOVE MATTRESS, complete,
3 ft., 38s. ; 3 ft. 6 in., 43s. ; 4 ft., 48s. 6d. ; 4 ft. 6 in., 52s. 6d.
Price for the Patent Wire Wove Mattress, without Bedstead—
3 ft., 9s. 6d. ; 3 ft. 6 in., 10s. 9d. ; 4 ft., 11s. 9d. ; 4 ft. 6 in., 12s. 9d.

For the Victorian woman, the bedroom was a valued space, functioning like a second, more private living room, with a chair set aside for sewing or reading and a desk for writing letters. In a more affluent household, this seating area might have been in an adjoining dressing room, a space that was expected to become a nursery. Her husband had his own bedroom, with a connecting door between the two. In smaller homes, bedrooms would have been shared or lodgers taken in to make ends meet, so there was far less chance of privacy.

The design of beds evolved throughout the century. For the wealthy, the early Victorian bed was a four-poster, or a half-tester with curtains drawn around the head of the bed. In 1881, however, Robert Edis, author of the Victorian style bible *Decoration and Furniture of Town Houses*, declared that the canopied four-poster was an outdated 'monstrosity', a dust trap that hindered the flow of fresh air. It was gradually replaced by the brass bed frame, which could be polished to a reassuringly clean shine. With curtained beds falling out of fashion, decorative folding screens became popular, giving a modicum of privacy along with a degree of insulation against draughts. Thick carpets, too, were discouraged, as they accumulated dust, and smaller rugs that could be taken up and beaten regularly were preferred.

Bed shapes changed once more towards the end of the century, as the Arts and Crafts aesthetic ushered in more restrained styles that were crafted in oak and sparingly carved. Other items of freestanding furniture would have included a dressing table and a wooden washstand with a marble top and a ceramic bowl decorated with pretty motifs, a tradition that only began to fade when plumbed-in bathrooms became more widespread.

Robert Edis also had strong views about wall decoration, recommending light colours or pleasantly nondescript patterns. In any case, green wallpapers were treated with suspicion when rumours about toxic dyes spread (see p. 160), but his objection to bright or bold wallpapers was more emotional. Edis believed symmetrical arrangements of flowers and fruit and particularly 'flights of birds' could overstimulate the imagination and cause all manner of fevered dreams.

The bedroom was a valued space for the Victorian woman, functioning like a more private living room, with a chair for sewing or reading, and a desk for writing letters.

ABOVE
William Morris's patterns – shown here are 'Willow Boughs', 'Strawberry Thief' and 'Trellis' – now speak of tradition, but many Victorians found them overly stylized.

OPPOSITE
Leanne von Arx's style recalls how a Victorian woman's bedroom doubled as a sitting room.

A STYLISH SANCTUARY

Paint shades can bring a strong look to bedrooms, but patterns reign supreme, whether on wallpapers, fabrics or upholstery.

ABOVE
Mid-century treasures in Fred Musik's dramatic scheme.

OPPOSITE
Geometric paint patterns add energy to a guest bedroom designed by Emilie Fournet.

Today, it feels more important than ever that our bedrooms foster a sense of escapism, whether that feeling comes from pared-back minimalism or fanciful patterns that would have had Robert Edis reaching for the smelling salts. The maximalist trend has played a part in reviving and reinterpreting 19th-century wallpapers, which might not have originally been intended for the bedroom, but nonetheless are brilliant for creating a patterned cocoon.

Over the past decade, luxury hotel design has had a huge influence on bedroom decor. Many a weekend mini-break has sparked a yearning for a freestanding bath in the bedroom, a feature that the Victorians probably thought they had waved goodbye to with the arrival of the first plumbed-in bathrooms. In some ways, interior designer Tiffany Duggan's bedroom suite harks back to its Victorian roots, with its freestanding bath, dressing room and seating area, but she has also worked in plenty of style twists to keep the whole space feeling contemporary (p. 156). In Kent, Samantha Bruce also favours a bath in the bedroom, but has gone for more of a French boudoir feel (p. 162).

Paint shades can bring a strong look to a bedroom, but patterns still reign supreme, whether on wallpapers, fabrics or upholstery – or on all three. As a palette cleanser, Helen Magowan's open-plan sleeping area is an adventure in space, fabric and structure that is innovative yet utterly serene (p. 172).

HOTEL STYLE BROUGHT HOME

For her master bedroom, interior designer Tiffany Duggan included plenty of elements that were mainstays of its Victorian predecessor, cleverly reinterpreting them for modern living. The focal point is a bed by Vielle + Frances, which has the look of a simplified rework of a traditional four-poster, its outline subtly echoing the original mouldings on the ceiling. The walls are papered in a design by Fromental with hints of Chinoiserie, its key tones repeated as punchier versions elsewhere in the room. The dark yellow reappears on the thick velvet curtains, and the red is picked up in the glossy bamboo-style furniture – another contemporary tribute to Victorian style and its fascination with all things oriental.

BELOW LEFT
A fluted chest from Tiffany's own company Trove echoes the Victorian fascination with bamboo furniture.

BELOW
A chair is illuminated by a 1970s rattan and brass floor lamp.

OPPOSITE
The ceiling mouldings feel integrated into a decorative yet innovative scheme.

BELOW
The metal-framed mirror is a French vintage find.

OPPOSITE
The hallway is painted in a deep, dark blue, contrasting with the bedroom's airy shades.

Tiffany turned the whole of the first floor into a proper hotel-style suite, converting the adjacent bedroom into a dressing room, with a shower and a loo concealed behind twin reeded glass doors. The in-bedroom bath is slightly smaller than usual, so that it fits comfortably in the recess of the bay window, with thick, velvet curtains offering complete privacy. The bath's exterior can be repainted, and its latest incarnation echoes the mellow yellow of the fabric. Modern textures, including the cast-concrete basin and brass trim on the wardrobes, along with the reeded glass, keep this scheme feeling contemporary.

Final touches – such as the racy tiger-print fabric used on a bench at the foot of the bed – are reminders that this is a space that indulges Victorian-inspired flights of fancy, but is also part of a larger family home, full of punchy style statements and design ideas.

BELOW
A kaleidoscope of wallpaper patterns in Solange Azagury-Partridge's home.

BELOW RIGHT
'Pimpernel', a Morris & Co. design, adds charm in Leanne Chandler's converted barn.

OPPOSITE
'Malachite' by Fornasetti from Cole & Son suits the modern Victorian feel of Linda Allen's home.

THE LETHAL APPEAL OF WALLPAPER

Over the course of the Victorian period, wallpaper went from being the preserve of the elite to a mass-produced product. Some designs contained the green pigment 'Scheele's Green', a copper arsenite that was highly toxic. Rumours about its dangers were rife, but it wasn't until 1862 when Dr Thomas Orton publicized the link between green wallpaper and the death of several children that the risks were taken more seriously.

In 1879, Queen Victoria reportedly had all of the green wallpaper in Buckingham Palace stripped out as a precaution after a visitor was taken ill, and by the 1880s, many wallpaper manufacturers had changed their formulas and advertised their wares as 'free from arsenic'.

AN ESCAPIST BOUDOIR

Old-school glamour reigns in Samantha Bruce's master bedroom in Kent, where vintage finds sit against dark paintwork and evocative fabrics. Window surrounds are painted in 'Downpipe' by Farrow & Ball, a steely grey shade that complements curtains in House of Hackney's 'Inferno' pattern. A wallpaper design by Deborah Bowness hangs over the bed, adding to the feel of a starlet's dressing room, complete with a petite vintage dressing table. Samantha has followed in her Victorian predecessors' footsteps by fitting a freestanding copper tub in the bedroom – except that her version is topped by a pink neon light spelling out 'Heaven'.

OPPOSITE
The hallway's two-tone paint effect helps to update the setting.

BELOW
A travelling trunk that folds out into a dressing table adds to the glamorous feel.

A spectacular French mirror stands propped up on the floor; to the left and behind a partition wall lies a dressing area and storage for clothes. The bedroom is unapologetically indulgent, but Samantha has toned things down a little with her choice of lighting: dainty modern pendants by Dyke & Dean. A chandelier might have been a step too far, even in this glamorous space. Most pieces, including the brass and marble bedside tables, were bought in junk shops in nearby Hastings, East Sussex, while the mirror was bought on an early morning trawl of antiques markets in France. By boldly mixing eras, Samantha has brought a luxuriously louche feel to this private space.

OPPOSITE
Extravagant curtains from House of Hackney hang next to the faux swags of a wallpaper design by Deborah Bowness.

RIGHT
An area for clothes storage lies behind the wall to the left of the bath.

IN PRAISE OF CHINTZ

'Chintz', derived from the Hindi *chint*, meaning 'sprinkle' or 'spray', has become shorthand for any slightly old-fashioned floral pattern. After Portuguese and Dutch colonists brought these fabrics back to Europe, the craze for such patterns reached a peak in the 17th century. Two hundred years later, British factories were churning out cheaper and fussier versions. Victorians loved furnishing with chintz with a smooth finish, favouring it over velvet and brocade, which were magnets for dust. The style was championed by Colefax & Fowler in the 1940s, revived in the 1970s and was popular into the 1980s. Despite Ikea urging everyone to 'chuck out your chintz' in 1996, it is now firmly back in favour, beefing up maximalist schemes or adding a nostalgic air to country homes.

ABOVE
The 'Nympheus' wallpaper by GP & J Baker is based on a Ming dynasty silk scroll.

OPPOSITE, TOP LEFT
A modern take on florals by Mònica Subidé for Soler in Alex and Mishari Al-Bader's home.

OPPOSITE, TOP RIGHT
The vintage Morris & Co. curtain at Spinks Nest was an eBay find.

OPPOSITE, BOTTOM LEFT
An antique chair in Suzanne Sharp's bedroom is covered in 'Avalon' by Bennison Fabrics.

OPPOSITE, BOTTOM RIGHT
A kantha quilt and embroidered cushions in Rebecca Gordon's guest bedroom.

BELOW
Blankets are from Melin Tregwynt and Abraham Moon, weaving mills with 19th-century roots.

BELOW RIGHT
The neat desk and red chair are by contemporary crafters Another Country.

OPPOSITE
Amanda made the ceramic lamp base; the bedside table is from Pinch.

A SPACE THAT FOSTERS CREATIVITY

It is fitting that Amanda Bannister chose a Morris & Co. wallpaper for the bedroom, as her entire home is furnished in the spirit of the Arts and Crafts movement. Believed to have been built for the village's Baptist minister, her 19th-century house is filled with handcrafted pieces by cabinetmakers, artists and ceramicists. The wallpaper is in a pattern called 'Seaweed', designed by John Henry Dearle in 1890, and foreshadows Art Nouveau with its sinuous curves.

A dado of tongue-and-groove panelling is painted in a soft blue, and the bed is upholstered in a similarly calm shade, with minimal decoration – apart from the rows of upholstery studs – so that it doesn't fight with the pattern on the walls. The wallpaper rises to meet the honey-toned stone above the bed, a reminder of the house's reassuringly solid presence and history.

RIGHT
Designs such as 'Allure' by Graham & Brown have an overblown appeal.

OPPOSITE
Wallpapers with a traditional feel still exude charm, while modern remixes inject a more energetic mood.

THE RETURN OF PATTERN

The wallpaper designs of Morris & Co. have become synonymous with the decor of the late Victorian period, and its patterns have been revived at regular intervals ever since. In the right context, these instantly recognizable designs can look fresh all over again – a fact that the company took on board. Following licensing deals, the patterns were retinted by Sanderson in the 1960s; more recent collaborations include Ben Pentreath and House of Hackney. Under Pentreath's direction, favourite designs were recast in dazzling hues, producing the perfect example of a Victorian Modern remix.

Other designers have also delved into the past for inspiration, taking the era's blowsy florals, botanical outlines and saturated colours as their starting point. While the living-room feature wall has fallen out of favour, in the bedroom a solid wall of pattern can work behind the headboard or along a side wall, if a wraparound pattern on all four sides would feel overwhelming.

'Blooming
 Marvellous',
 Divine Savages
'Farmhouse Floral',
 Deborah Bowness
'Pimpernel',
 Morris & Co.

'Stapleton Park',
 Sanderson
'Strawberry Thief',
 Morris & Co
'Bryher Rose',
 House of Hackney

'Money Tree',
 Poodle & Blonde
'Willow Boughs',
 Morris & Co.,
 coloured by
 Ben Pentreath
'Food Babies',
 Poodle & Blonde

'Golden Lily',
 House of Hackney,
 orignally created
 by Morris & Co.
'Zeus',
 House of Hackney
'Ava Marika',
 Woodchip &
 Magnolia

TRANSFORMED BY ARCHITECTURE

At the end of the 19th century, this terraced house in London had a draper's shop on the ground floor. With the shop long gone, the interior has been opened up to create voids and double-height spaces traversed by a staircase – and giant ribbons of fabric, threaded through the entire house in a tribute to its textiles-trading past. The woven theme also chimed with owner Helen Magowan, who is a creative director working with textiles.

In the top-floor bedroom, the embroidered and pleated ribbons begin their journey, before dropping down through the other floors, looped and twisted like giant Christmas garlands. Functioning as a gigantic work of art, these lengths of fabric are the creation of textile artists Deepa Panchamia and Anna Glover.

BELOW LEFT
An internal room called the 'sewing box' contains a dressing room and bathroom, with a studio above.

BELOW
The staircase acts as a loom-like frame to guide the ribbons down to the lower floors.

OPPOSITE
Architecture meets art in a design that pays tribute to the house's 19th-century occupants.

OPPOSITE
Once a series of closed-off rooms, this
terraced house is now a flowing space.

BELOW
Images and motifs tell the story of the
Roberts family, who ran a draper's shop here.

Patrick Lewis Architects dreamed up this adventure in space, light, cloth and structure, which includes an internal box of a room within the bedroom. Inside this oak and larch structure lies the bathroom and dressing room, with a work studio above, reached by external stairs. From inside, Helen can peep down into the bedroom through a hinged wooden window.

For the architect, this project was about turning the small, closed-off rooms into something as laterally open as possible. The challenge was all the greater because the house had been divided into two flats in a former life, which made its rooms even darker. The result shows how the spirit of open-plan living can be achieved, even within the limited proportions of a Victorian terraced house.

WAYS WITH CHILDREN'S ROOMS

The key to designing and then decorating a child's bedroom is to think ahead: nursery motifs that are charming in a baby's room are soon outgrown, while a paint shade that works for a nine-year-old child runs the risk of being deemed uncool once that child becomes a teenager. A better bet is to add bright colours in the form of throws, rugs or framed prints, items that can be changed more easily than hanging new wallpaper. Stripes or geometric patterns have a timelessness to them, while beds that are raised or feel like a secret hideaway will always feel special. Vintage furniture is a good choice for a child's room, especially if you can find inexpensive pieces in charity shops. Toy storage is essential, whether in the form of baskets, chest or shelves, and a desk will come into its own once homework can be done without help.

OPPOSITE, TOP LEFT
Susannah Parker mixes vintage finds for
a nursery mood.

OPPOSITE, TOP RIGHT
Fred Musik's cool shades and floor-level
lounging would tick most teenagers' boxes.

OPPOSITE, BOTTOM LEFT
Sharp angles and a wall-mounted tube light
define a bedroom in Annabel White's home.

OPPOSITE, BOTTOM RIGHT
'Florica' wallpaper by Harlequin feels
nostalgic for Mairead Turner's daughter.

RIGHT
The cosy box bed was built specially for
Lucy Russell's home in the Cotswolds.

OVERLEAF
Pandora Sykes created a dreamy hideaway
with 'Improvisation' wallpaper by Ottoline.

BATHROOMS

Although the Victorians gave us the claw-foot bath – and even an early version of the power shower – their concept of bathing had more to do with health and hygiene than with pleasure, and bathrooms were small and functional. Modern homeowners have found innovative ways to deal with these inherited spaces, whether through decoration or by joining rooms together to make a spacious family bathroom. Either way, contemporary versions incorporate pattern, colour and texture to create luxurious spaces for lingering in.

ON P. 180
Architect Z He evokes Renaissance inspiration in tile form.

OPPOSITE
A freestanding tub under the roof beams of Lucy Russell's former schoolhouse in the Cotswolds.

BELOW
By the 1890s, baths could be embellished, but for the most part were still filled by hand. Shanks & Co. catalogue, 1896.

THE ERA OF INVENTION

SHANKS & Cº BARRHEAD NEAR GLASGOW   10

SHANKS' HIGH CLASS — BATH DECORATIONS — SUITABLE FOR ALL KINDS OF BATHS.

DESIGN A.   DESIGN B.
DESIGN C.   DESIGN D.
DESIGN E.   DESIGN F.

These illustrate a few of our Designs, but any scheme of Colouring can be adapted to the various patterns as may be desired. Special Designs on application.

At the start of the Victorian era, the idea of having hot water on tap was a distant dream. 'Taking a bath' meant sitting in a tub by the fire that was filled and emptied by hand. For the wealthy, this would have taken place in an upstairs bedroom or dressing room, but in a working-class home a tub would have been found in the back living room, with the same water used and reused by every member of the family, oldest to youngest (the origins of the phrase 'throwing the baby out with the bath water').

But even for the rich, taking a bath wasn't the lie-back-and-relax experience it is today. Water cooled swiftly as soon as it hit the tub, and some upper-class women might have worn a modesty shift – like a voluminous nightdress – for the duration. When the first plumbed-in bathrooms arrived in the late 1870s, they were the preserve of the very wealthy and looked rather like furnished rooms, complete with wallpaper, curtains and rugs. The bath, basin and WC were encased in hulking mahogany frames, so they resembled large pieces of furniture; in the case of the WC, this helped disguise its true function.

By the 1880s, improved mains drainage and the arrival of in-room gas water heaters (the Geyser was a leading model) meant that builders began to include a bathroom and indoor toilet on floorplans of new houses aimed firmly at the middle classes. Even so, these rooms were small and spartan, with the emphasis on hygiene, rather than decor.

The new fashion was for a basin or bath to be mounted on a pedestal or feet, so that the floor around them could be mopped efficiently. The consumer public was now far more aware of 'invisible' germs, and favoured materials such as porcelain or enamel for their reassuringly clean shine. Walls also began to be clad in plain porcelain tiles or 'sanitary' wallpaper, and floors were covered in newly invented linoleum.

Even for the wealthy, taking a bath wasn't the relaxing experience it is today, and some women might have worn a modesty shift for the duration.

The Victorians at the close of the century couldn't resist their love of pattern for long, and more florid designs gradually crept onto the surfaces of porcelain tiles and fittings. During the 1890s, catalogues from companies such as Shanks & Co. (p. 183) and Twyford (p. 190) pictured baths, basins and toilets that were lavishly decorated with floral motifs.

In a Victorian semi that has inherited one of these comparatively small bathrooms, creative solutions can make the most of every inch of the space available. One popular alternative has been to commandeer a neighbouring bedroom for a more spacious bathing experience; another option is to add a second bathroom in a loft extension, where there is scope to plan a layout from scratch, including a space-saving shower.

LEFT
William De Morgan's glazed tiles were the preserve of wealthy Victorians.

OPPOSITE
A William Holland tub has a historic feel in Francesca Rowan Plowden's interior design for Kingshill Farmhouse in Kent.

A LUXURIOUS RETREAT

Bold colours or a vintage centrepiece help to give small bathrooms and loos a strong identity, while scaled-down fittings can work wonders.

ABOVE
Interesting colour combinations make Sandra Barrio von Hurter's en suite an inviting space.

OPPOSITE
Christian Haas's modern en suite with an 'Ultrafragola' mirror designed by Ettore Sottsass and Sori Yanagi's 'Butterfly' stool.

Because of their small size, bathrooms offer the perfect opportunity to be adventurous with colour or pattern – with a striking wallpaper, for example, which would feel overwhelming in a larger room. In Devon, Susannah Parker used papers and fabrics by House of Hackney, a company that has helped revive our modern love of Victoriana (p. 192). Today's efficient heating and ventilation systems mean that it is usually fine to hang wallpaper in a bathroom; a couple of coats of clear varnish or a sheet of clear Perspex will add extra protection from splashes.

Tiles are a feature of most bathrooms, and the geometric patterns that delighted the Victorians are still going strong or have been updated in interesting ways. Companies such as Surface View can even reproduce works of art from the collections of the Victoria and Albert Museum, the Ashmolean and the National Portrait Gallery as a set of printed tiles (see pp. 180, 206).

In terms of lighting, whatever type of fitting you choose – whether a pendant light, wall sconces, task lighting around a mirror or all three – must have the correct IP rating (for 'ingress protection', indicating how close it can be to a water source). For her bath-in-a-bedroom area in East Sussex, Scarlett Gowing opted for contemporary Italian lighting to highlight the grandeur of her Grade II-listed home (p. 188). Bold colours or a vintage centrepiece will work equally well to give smaller bathrooms and loos a strong identity, while scaled-down fittings can work wonders (p. 198).

A BATH WITH A VIEW

When Scarlett Gowing and her husband Josh (see also p. 26) took on this rambling mansion in East Sussex, they went back to the original floorplans to create a family-friendly layout. The sheer scale of this master bedroom/bathing area meant that solutions had to be big and bold, so Scarlett chose a clean-lined modern bath by Clearwater as the centrepiece. It stands on a raised area (which conceals all the pipework) under a stained-glass window. The lighting by Cristina Celestino for Esperia Luci also has enough presence to occupy the large, airy space.

Having spent many years working in fashion, textures are important to Scarlett, from the deep pile of the velvet curtains and rug to the marble in the seating area. A separate WC, hidden behind a door, also benefits from plenty of luxe touches, including a vintage Lucite mirror and cool brassware.

ABOVE
A contemporary chandelier draws the eye up to the original stained-glass windows.

LEFT
A seating area with Warren Platner chairs for Knoll. A dressing room lies beyond the door.

OPPOSITE
The bath's silhouette exudes modern luxury, but in a historic setting.

THE EVOLUTION OF THE LOO

The traditional high-level cistern loo is making a comeback, with companies such as Catchpole & Rye producing them in a range of metal finishes and colours. The design wasn't an overnight success when first invented, however. The gushing water seemed alarmingly loud – with the added worry that the sound made it all-too obvious what was going on behind that locked door. In modern bathrooms, traditional shapes and more streamlined silhouettes are popular, but the lavishly decorated loos of the late Victorian period are yet to enjoy a full revival (below).

BELOW LEFT
By the end of the 19th century, decorative flourishes were available on every bathroom surface. Twyford catalogue, 1894.

BELOW
A high-cistern loo is prettified by wallpaper from Pip Studio and a pink cement basin in Leanne Chandler's home.

OPPOSITE, TOP LEFT
Utilitarian fittings meet decorative tiles in Field Day Studio's design.

OPPOSITE, TOP RIGHT
Moroccan *zellige* tiles add gloss to traditional fittings in Jo Berryman's home.

OPPOSITE, BELOW LEFT
A salvaged 1970s loo in sunshine yellow in Sarah Heaton's converted 19th-century jail.

OPPOSITE, BELOW RIGHT
Emily Huc chose a modern loo, but customized a vintage washstand for the sink.

Designs of the "Twycliffe" Patent Syphon Closet Basin.

No. 2—Plain Surface, White or Ivory, 50/-

"Corinthian" Pattern, in Relief.
No. 4—With Slop Top, White or Ivory, 75/-
No. 1—Without „ 54/-

No. 3—Strong Fire Clay. Enamelled inside, 44/-

"Poppy," Printed.
No. 26—Blue on White Ware } 58/6
No. 27—Brown on Ivory Ware

"Cactus," Printed and Coloured.
No. 33—Brown on Ivory Ware, 78/6

"Mikado," Printed.
No. 28—Blue on White Ware } 58/6
No. 29—Brown on Ivory Ware

"Japanesque," Printed.
No. 30—Blue on White Ware } 58/6
No. 31—Brown on Ivory Ware

"Corinthian" Pattern, in Relief.
No. 25—Blue and Gold, 136/-

"Cactus," Printed.
No. 32—Brown on Ivory Ware, 58/6

6 A

IMMERSIVE PATTERNS AND COLOURS

In Devon, interior designer Susannah Parker used moody hues and evocative patterns for her en suite, in what would have originally been an adjoining bedroom. She chose wallpaper in 'Limerence' from House of Hackney to create an immersive 'bottom-of-the-lake' feeling. It's a pattern that draws on the best Victorian traditions, bumped up with intense colours. Susannah used the design in two different colourways: 'Ink' for the wallpaper in the bedroom, and 'Quartz Pink' for the fabric of the blind in the bathroom, which echoes the dusky shade of paint – 'Brinjal' by Farrow & Ball – on the exterior of the bath, subtle repetitions that ensure the maximalist scheme feels cohesive.

OPPOSITE
The fireplace, mirror and chair recall how early Victorian bathrooms were furnished.

BELOW LEFT
Vintage mirrors reflect modern lighting shapes.

BELOW
Bedroom walls papered in House of Hackney's 'Limerence' set the scene.

When the family moved into the rectory, it was quickly apparent that very few walls or floors were straight. Susannah's design for the interior and the renovations had to work around the building's many quirks, a common issue in 19th-century homes. The floor of the new en suite, for example, had to be levelled so that tiles could be laid without developing cracks – the change in horizontal levels is just visible at the doorway. The family bathroom has a more playful mood, with scampering monkeys, a vintage painting and a bath painted to match the wallpaper. Black herringbone floor tiles and woodwork keep the look grounded.

RIGHT
Collectibles continue the wildlife theme of the wallpaper from House of Hackney.

OPPOSITE
A traditional basin from Victorian Plumbing is a good match for the Aston Matthews bath.

AN IRIDESCENT SHADE
IN A SMALL SPACE

The conversion of a 19th-century outbuilding in Norfolk, owned by Ana Perez and called Spinks Nest, led to the creation of this very petite bathroom decorated in a bold, glossy shade of green ('Jewel Beetle' by Little Greene). Against the reclaimed fittings and bespoke carpentry, the vivid colour brings the space to life, and shines out against the chalky black limewash. A wide, shallow basin is mounted on a bespoke cabinet in reclaimed iroko by design team Ridge & Furrow; the same wood was used for the toilet seat and surround. Opposite the loo, with a reconditioned cistern from a reclamation yard, there is just enough space for a shower, lined in grey microcement and made deep enough to double as a bath. This bathroom is a perfect example of what can be achieved in a small space, where every inch counts and being bland is not an option.

BELOW LEFT
The glossy green is repeated on the ceiling of the shower/tub for an extra hit of colour.

BELOW
The bathroom lies off the hallway, clad in tongue-and-groove panelling.

OPPOSITE
Foliage and a vintage painting evoke potting-shed chic.

THE SMALLEST ROOM

A compact bathroom can benefit from specialist fittings, but its small size also presents an opportunity for some creative solutions. Choosing a shorter-than-average bath is a sensible option, but if the combination of bath, loo and basin is still looking too cramped, try setting the bath at an angle. In a long, narrow room, a deep Japanese-style soaking tub is a particularly good use of floor space, especially when paired with a matching basin and dado panelling to give coherence to the room.

There are plenty of slimline basins to choose from; as a general rule, the more floor that is visible, the larger a room will appear, so if space is an issue, opt for a wall-mounted basin over a pedestal style. A wide basin design that provides an extra surface for toiletries is another space-saver. If your budget doesn't extend to refitting the bathroom, paint is a simple but effective way to add impact by injecting colour, a glossy texture or a subtle paint effect.

RIGHT
Suzanne Sharp stencilled faux panelling
shapes onto the walls.

OPPOSITE, TOP LEFT
Architect Z He's deep, Japanese-style soaking
tub is a great use of floorspace.

OPPOSITE, TOP RIGHT
A slimline, wide basin saves space and adds
storage in Siri Zanelli's loft en suite.

OPPOSITE, BOTTOM LEFT
'Boiled Egg' paint from Plain English brings
zing to this small space by Michaelis Boyd.

OPPOSITE, BOTTOM RIGHT
Jo Berryman positioned this short bath
at an angle for a more creative layout.

A MEETING OF GLAMOROUS ELEMENTS

Make-up artist Lisa Valencia has seen more than her fair share of stylish locations. Back at home, her bathroom provided an opportunity to create timeless glamour, bringing together luxurious materials and vintage finds. The centrepiece is a high-sheen copper bath by William Holland; above is a photograph by Lisa's husband John Rowley, a fashion and beauty photographer. The basin is a reclamation-yard find, and came complete with gold taps for a touch of Hollywood Regency opulence; the floor is covered with a modern interpretation of classic Victorian encaustic tiles.

Storage for a selection of beauty products is a must, and a vintage wall cabinet ticks that box. Walls in polished grey plaster provide a suitable backdrop to these stand-out pieces. For Lisa and John, who travel extensively for work, this mix of styles gives them the 'at home' feeling they crave.

BELOW LEFT
A William Holland bath in copper is a deep and shiny centrepiece.

BELOW
Wall lights with an industrial feel tone down the extravagance of the marble basin.

OPPOSITE
John's photograph of the model Lenka makes this space feel ever-modern.

MIXING RUSTIC TEXTURES

Leanne Chandler's home in the Kent countryside comprises three farm buildings: a 19th-century barn at the centre, bookended by two later additions, a stable and a garage. The family bathroom (overleaf) is in the oldest part of the house, and there is also an en suite (opposite and below).

In the en suite, Leanne added tongue-and-groove panelling to the walls, while bright-blue floor tiles, vintage shelving and a large macramé pendant light above the bath all contribute to the holiday mood. The bath taps and towel rail are made from lengths of copper piping, and complement the freestanding, handcrafted copper bath from London Encaustic.

OPPOSITE
Garden tap valves and a length of copper piping have been turned into a simple tap.

BELOW LEFT
The stud wall between bedroom and bathroom is clad with wood panelling on both sides.

BELOW
An extra-wide basin from Holloways of Ludlow maintains marital harmony on busy mornings.

The family bathroom has retained the weathered timber cladding from its previous incarnation as a barn. These original boards are partnered with plain modern planks, laid horizontally and painted white. Two enamel basins with black taps appealed to Leanne's love of all things monochrome; the bath filler is made from copper piping and valves, as in the en suite. This bathroom is mostly used by the couple's two sons, so Leanne aimed for more of a cabin feel, with wall-mounted ship's lights and a rustic stools.

RIGHT
The copper verdigris patina feels both age-old and vibrant.

OPPOSITE
Bare surfaces celebrate, rather than disguise, the building's original use.

TIMELESS TILES

Many Victorian tile designs that endure today were, in turn, influenced by Islamic traditions. In 1872, William De Morgan was commissioned to replicate 15th- and 16th-century tiles from Turkey, Egypt and Syria for the Arab Hall at Leighton House, London, an experience that contributed to his distinctively florid style, with its rich palette of blues, greens and gold.

The Victorian fascination with geometric tessellations had been gathering pace since architect and designer Owen Jones published studies of the intricate tiles of the Alhambra in Andalusia, Spain, in the 1840s. He declared that the patterns found within the medieval fortress offered infinite possibilities for design and colour, which are still being explored today.

BELOW LEFT
Vibrant handpainted Mexican tiles in Steph Wilson's home in a former school.

BELOW
Paolo Veronese's *Happy Union* (1575), reproduced in tiles from Surface View.

OPPOSITE
Modern tiles still echo popular Victorian designs, many of which were themselves inspired by Islamic traditions.

OVERLEAF
A wraparound grid of tiles in Joe Barton's Brighton home by Field Day Studio.

'Dyrham Dairy',
National Trust
Tile Collection
by Ca' Pietra
'Old Faro',
Lapicida
'Aurelia',
New Ravenna

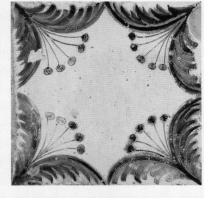

'Chinoiserie',
New Ravenna
'Atlas',
Neisha Crosland
for Fired Earth
'Laurette',
Maison Bahya

'Trädgård',
Marrakech Design
'Versailles',
Marrakech Design
'Marseilles',
Marrakech Design

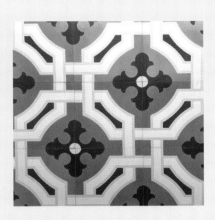

'Egrets',
New Ravenna
'Safi',
Maison Bahya
'Bossa',
Mini Labo for
Maison Bahya

WORKSPACES

A book-lined library was the aspiration of many a middle-class Victorian gentleman, decorated to make it abundantly clear that this was where Very Important Things happened – even if all that really meant was reading the newspaper in peace. For most women, however, a room to call her own was still a distant dream. Today, of course, working from home has become the norm for many of us, whether that involves a full-fledged home office or setting up a corner in a larger room.

ON P. 210
Calm symmetry in a home in Chicago,
Illinois, by Jen Talbot Design, with
a chandelier from Kelly Wearstler.

OPPOSITE
Vintage collections in a writing corner
of Suzanne Sharp's London home.

BELOW
Advertisement for 'superior' furniture to
furnish a home library. Oetzmann & Co.,
c. 1880s.

SCHOLARLY PURSUITS

At the beginning of the Victorian era, in the 1830s and '40s,
a gentleman's study was the preserve of the wealthy, with books
being relatively expensive objects. But as advances in printing
brought books and pamphlets within the reach of the middle
classes, the idea of a room dedicated to reading and study
became an achievable aspiration.

In modest homes, the library often doubled as the family's
dining room, but in large townhouses or country piles it was
a dedicated space, its rarefied atmosphere conveyed through
the inclusion of wood panelling, marble fireplaces and many
bookshelves. Bespoke bookcases, sometimes topped with
pediments or Gothic arches, would have been made by a
carpenter to designs seen in a pattern book or duplicated to
complement an existing piece. If hardwood was too expensive,
then cheaper timber could be given a wood stain to get the look.

The Victorian library or dining room would have been lit
by oil lamps, which would feel very dim and inefficient today.
Oil lamps were also pretty noxious things, particularly before
the invention of a metal mesh net that fitted over the flame
and made it easier to control. Paraffin and gas lamps were also
available towards the latter half of the century. By the end of
it, many Victorian homes would have had a mix of light sources,
as well as candles.

In a house that had a gas supply installed, wall sconces were
often fitted on either side of an overmantel mirror, which helped
to amplify and reflect the light into the room. An additional
desk lamp could be fed with a flexible gas tube – a design
that seems alarmingly dangerous to us today. Gas lighting
was gradually snuffed out by the advent of mains electricity
in the early 1900s, along with the invention of the filament
bulb, whose glow was so unusually bright that a whole raft of

BELOW
Volumes in a Victorian library were bound in leather or decorated with marbled papers.

OPPOSITE
Three sources of lighting in Jos White's home office make it a hardworking space.

lampshade designs sprang up, deflecting the intense light in suitably fashionable ways.

It is less likely that these advances would have trickled down to working-class homes, where 'working from home' had long been a fact of life – although in a rather different context. Women and children took in piecework, such as sewing, and many family businesses continued to be run from the home. There was no question of setting aside a separate room for such activities; the work was simply carried out wherever possible, alongside other chores.

In the 21st-century home, history is repeated as workspaces are often slotted into any room with enough space, from the dining room – particularly where a kitchen-diner extension has been added at the back – to the smallest bedroom or a corner of a loft extension, at a slight remove from the busy activity of life downstairs.

For the Victorians, the gentleman's study was the preserve of the wealthy, as books were relatively expensive and precious objects.

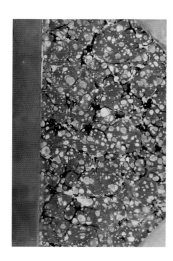

THE HOME OFFICE

In the Modern Victorian home, rooms that have
been converted into flexible workspaces can
be easily transformed back to their original use.

ABOVE
A French steel desk forms a gleaming
centrepiece in a study designed by
Tricia Cunningham.

OPPOSITE
Vintage shopfront letters spell out
a motivational message in Samantha
Bruce's colourful home.

A home office has to be designed with the practicalities of work
in mind. Ideally, it will connect to the rest of the home in terms
of style while still feeling like a calm hideaway, a place where you
are surrounded by inspiring objects and reference tools that help
you focus on the job in hand. That's the dream, anyway – but the
widespread move to home-working during the pandemic and
beyond has shown us that work can be done almost anywhere,
provided there is a bit of space and good WiFi.

Home offices that have plenty of character provide a place to
both work and let inspiration flow. In Brighton, a former bedroom
has been transformed into the ideal space for fostering creativity
(p. 218), and a little-used dining room now earns its keep in northern
Wales (p. 226). In West Sussex, an area that was once a servants'
entrance and scullery is now a home office (p. 220), and in Highgate,
North London, a front room was turned into a dual workspace during
lockdown, and has stayed that way ever since (p. 222).

Importantly, these are flexible spaces that can be easily
converted back to their original use. For more long-term solutions,
clever architectural room dividers can be called into service to
separate off a portion of an open-plan living space (p. 232). All of
which goes to show how the Victorian home can be constantly
adapted in creative ways to suit ever-changing needs.

A CLEAR FOCUS

The wraparound shade of green used on the walls and ceiling in screenwriter Joe Barton's home office in Brighton, West Sussex, is strong enough to give the room a distinct identity without overwhelming it. The paint links with other bold colours dotted throughout the house – a mellow yellow in the kitchen and a warm orange in the bathroom, for example (pp. 134, 208–9).

To transform this room, which would have originally been a small bedroom or a dressing room for the master bedroom next door, Joe called on the services of interior-design firm Field Day Studio. The desk is set in the centre of the room, creating a feeling of spaciousness and a clear sense of purpose. The furniture feels classic, while lighting has a vintage mood, with an elegant Art Deco desk lamp and pendant in opaline glass, and a tripod floor lamp that is a nod to Joe's film and television career.

OPPOSITE
The paint shade, 'Verdigris' by Farrow & Ball, is taken across the ceiling for maximum impact.

BELOW LEFT
Industrial-style shelving made from scaffolding planks keeps books in order.

BELOW
A restored fireplace in the corner is a reminder of the room's Victorian roots.

A HALLWAY RECLAIMED

Collette Vernon's home forms one-half of a manor house, a grand building with a Georgian core that was extended in the 19th century. Most of the rooms are large in scale, but this transitional area off the double-living room is more petite. A 'secret' door set into the panelling leads to a downstairs loo, indicating that the two rooms were probably once a scullery and tradesman's entrance.

The space has now been transformed into an office, where Collette runs her vintage and antique furniture business. Although the majority of her stock is in storage, a few favourite finds have made their way into the room, including a sofa by Matteo Thun, co-founder of the Memphis Group, for Rossi di Albizzate, which slots neatly under the stained-glass windows. A 'DSW' chair by Charles and Ray Eames sits in front of an oak desk; next to the sofa, a gilt mirror and brass drinks trolley reflect Collette's eclectic tastes.

BELOW LEFT
A lotus-flower lamp from Maison Jansen sits against delicately tinted stained glass.

BELOW
The dado panelling, complete with hidden door, is painted in 'Cornforth White' by Farrow & Ball.

OPPOSITE
Set between the living room and the kitchen, the space can also be used for reading or watching TV.

BELOW
Double-doors between the office and living room are painted in contrasting shades to emphasize the separation.

BELOW RIGHT
Hanging above a desk designed for co-working is a kimono, a reminder of the time Siri spent studying in Japan.

OPPOSITE
Walls have been painted in 'Soft Flamingo' by Pure & Original, with lighting from Flos and Isamu Noguchi.

A COLOURFUL DUAL WORKSPACE

During lockdown, architect Siri Zanelli turned her front room into an office for two. Her terraced Victorian home already had a snug seating area in the rear reception room, and a dining space had been incorporated into the extended kitchen at the back, so converting the front room into a workspace did not drastically change the family's day-to-day habits. Double-doors allow the working day to be shut away at night, and shelves and bespoke storage units in the alcoves and set into the window seat provide plenty of storage. The bold colour scheme was the result of a collaboration with KOI Colour Studio, with ecological clay-based paints giving the room a distinct personality. The result is a calm workspace – and the fact that it makes an attractive backdrop to Zoom calls is an added bonus.

THE VICTORIAN MODERN LIBRARY

The rise of affordable books, pamphlets and newspapers over the course of the Victorian period helped turn reading from a scholarly activity for the few into a leisure pursuit for the many. The most popular writer of fiction at the time was Charles Dickens, whose books were serialized in monthly instalments that were eagerly awaited and read aloud, allowing them to be enjoyed by everyone – including by those who couldn't read or afford their own books.

Today, a home library can take many forms, from a separate book-lined room to a dedicated set of shelves, neatly slotted into a hallway recess.

LEFT
In Lucy Russell's Cotswolds home, shelving continues above the door frame.

OPPOSITE, TOP LEFT
A recessed set of shelves on the landing provides a home for a small part of Pandora Sykes's collection of books.

OPPOSITE, TOP RIGHT
Kate Daudy takes an artistic approach to shelves, framing them with felt letters.

OPPOSITE, BOTTOM LEFT
Books and pops of colour add personality in Susannah Parker's home in Devon.

OPPOSITE, BOTTOM RIGHT
Sandra Barrio von Hurter's shelving is painted in 'Hunter Dunn' by Paint & Paper Library.

OPPOSITE
Floral prints in saturated shades feel funky, rather than fusty.

BELOW
A Victorian sampler works well against walls painted in 'Adventurer' by Little Greene.

BELOW RIGHT
A reupholstered armchair by the wood-burner provides a cosy reading nook.

A DINING ROOM REINVENTED

Interior designer Mairead Turner (see also p. 36) realized that the dining room of her Victorian home in Anglesey had a lot going for it. It had ample light, was set on the other side of the hall from the busy kitchen, and was rarely used. All of this made it the perfect location for her home office – a space where she has experimented with vivid paint colours, bold wallpaper and vintage furniture finds.

The desk is formed of two simple trestles from Ikea, topped with a piece of marble cut specially to echo the shape of the bay window. In front of it sits an Ercol dining chair, a junk-shop find. Walls have been painted in two calming shades, with wallpaper by Little Greene and Roman blinds in a vivid turquoise. Dusky pink ceramic tiles on the floor complement the paintbox colour palette; a rug can be added to warm up the space if needed. In the corner, a vintage armchair provides a spot for moments of reflection and inspiration.

CREATIVE SPACES

Creatives who work from home bring fresh ideas to workspaces, with rooms that dovetail practical considerations with strong style statements. Makers, designers and writers still need to have plenty of reference materials or equipment to hand, but these can be stored in myriad ways, from practical box files to drawers, units on wheels to vintage cabinets. A desk needn't be too 'officey' or industrial in feel, as long as it is comfortable and provides enough room to spread out paperwork, books, swatches of fabrics, or anything else that might be required.

Some workspaces might also need to include a second, smaller table for client meetings or presentations. Having plenty of leafy plants is always a good idea, and if there isn't a view outside the window, make your own with a gallery wall of pictures.

ABOVE LEFT
In Hannah Wright's home, a 1970s Swedish workbench is used for storage and as a desk.

ABOVE
Fleur Ward hung a striking wallpaper from Designers Guild to keep her feeling inspired.

OPPOSITE
Sandra Barrio von Hurter uses this desk for business admin, but the mood is far from grey.

OVERLEAF
With its glossy colours and stacks of fabrics, Suzanne Sharp's home office brims with ideas.

AN ELEGANT STRUCTURAL DIVIDER

In the London home of jewelry-maker Sheherazade Goldsmith, a glazed room-divider, reminiscent of the designs of Charles Rennie Mackintosh, has been inserted into the living room. It is a clever and elegant device that screens off Sheherazade's home office, while ensuring that she does not feel disconnected from family life while working. It also preserves a connection to the room's original scale and architecture.

Furniture is modern and pared back: the desk (actually a dining table from Italian company Tonelli Design) is a chic take on the trestle table, with sections crafted in glass. For the desk chair, a classic design by Charles and Ray Eames is both ergonomic and practical. One wall is covered in cork to make a super-sized pinboard, helping the space feel like a fully fledged design studio. Tear sheets, works-in-progress and ideas can be stuck on the wall, as reference points for Sheherazade's work as the co-founder of jewelry company Loquet, or simply to foster a feeling of bold creativity.

A wall light by Serge Mouille, another mid-century design classic, acts as a task lamp. The space is large enough to include a breakout seating area for meetings alongside the desk, which overlooks the garden, and shutters can be flipped down to aid focus.

RIGHT ABOVE
A pollen-yellow sofa in the living room contrasts with the strong lines of the divider.

RIGHT BELOW
The glazed screen lets natural light flow in, while creating some privacy.

OPPOSITE
A pinboard is used to keep track of current designs and gather ideas for the future.

OFFICE NOOKS

The Victorian gentleman could retire to his library and firmly close the door on the rest of the household, but for his modern counterpart that's not always possible, or even desirable. Sometimes all you need – or have space for – is a desk tucked away unobtrusively in a dining room, bedroom, even a kitchen, particularly if it was created hastily during lockdown. But there are ways to keep the space feeling separate, so that it functions as efficiently as possible. A small desk can be fitted into an alcove to one side of a fireplace, or slotted into a corner of a room, with shelving above to help separate it from the rest of the space.

Even a small gallery wall can define a home office within a larger room. A table doesn't need to be big or expensive: drop-sided versions save on space, and vintage or trestle tables are inexpensive options. If the office area is in the corner of a room, task lighting is important, both from a practical point of view and so that the space exists in its own pool of light.

ABOVE RIGHT
In this converted tannery, Howark Design built a bespoke desk for a tricky spot.

RIGHT
Chris Graves set a vintage table in a corner of the kitchen that is bathed in light.

OPPOSITE, TOP LEFT
Mary Mulryan turned the old entrance of her converted pub into a writing corner.

OPPOSITE, TOP RIGHT
Crisp whites work for this window-side desk in Christian Haas's home.

OPPOSITE, BELOW LEFT
A trio of pendants illuminates Emily Huc's small drop-sided table.

OPPOSITE, BELOW RIGHT
'String' shelving, first designed in 1949, helps define a corner of a guest bedroom as a workstation.

DIRECTORY & RESOURCES

HOMEOWNERS

Alex Al-Bader soler.co.uk
Linda Allen madforsquirrels.com
Solange Azagury-Partridge solange.co.uk
Amanda Bannister thecraftsmanscottage.com
Joe Barton twitter.com/JoeBarton
Jo Berryman joberryman.com
Sarah Brown sarahbrowninteriors.com
Danielle Bux @daniellebux
Louise Carlisle oysterinteriors.com
Lucinda Chambers collagerie.com
Leanne Chandler blossom-home.co.uk
Kate Daudy katedaudy.com
Tiffany Duggan studioduggan.com
Sam Godsal cobblerscove.com/the-hotel
Sheherazade Goldsmith loquetlondon.com
Rebecca Gordon rebeccagordonart.co.uk
Scarlett Gowing scarlettgowing.com
Chris Graves clarenceandgraves.com
Christian Haas christian-haas.com
Emily Huc lamaisonkensal.co.uk
Lisa Jewell instagram.com/lisajewelluk
Nikos Koulouras mathesonwhiteley.com
Afroditi Krassa afroditi.com
Christopher Lian christopherlian.com
Juan de Mayoralgo instagram.com/
juandemayoralgo
Lisa Mehydene edit58.com
Fred Musik fredmusik.com
Susannah Parker instagram.com/piperandpoet
Ana Perez spinksnest.com
Lucy Russell instagram.com/lucie.app
Suzanne Sharp suzannesharpstudio.com
Annie Sloan anniesloan.com
Pandora Sykes pandorasykes.com
Robert Storey storeystudio.com
Mairead Turner maireadandcointeriors.com
Lisa Valencia lisavalencia.com
Collette Vernon thevintagetrader.co.uk
Leanne von Arx vonarxstyle.com
Sandra Barrio von Hurter sandraalexandra.com
Fleur Ward ohhfleur.com
Patrick Williams berdoulat.co.uk
Steph Wilson steph-wilson.com
Hannah Wright ebtd.co.uk
Siri Zanelli collectiveworks.net
Z He instagram.com/z_yun_he

ARCHITECTS, ARTISTS AND INTERIOR DESIGNERS

Kate Arbuthnott katearbuthnottinteriors.co.uk
Berdoulat berdoulat.co.uk
BWArchitects Basil Walter, bw-architects.com
Clarence & Graves clarenceandgraves.com
Tricia Cunningham triciacunninghaminteriors.com
Field Day Studio fielddaystudio.com
Emilie Fournet emiliefournetinteriors.com
Anna Glover annaglover.co.uk
Howark Design howark-design.co.uk
Michaelis Boyd michaelisboyd.com
Nice Projects Simone McEwan, niceprojects.work
Deepa Panchamia deepapanchamia.com
Patrick Lewis Architects patricklewisarchitects.com
Ridge & Furrow ridgeandfurrow.co.uk
Francesca Rowan Plowden rowanplowden.com
Flora Soames florasoames.com
Jen Talbot jentalbotdesign.com
The Vawdrey House thevawdreyhouse.com
White Arrow thewhitearrow.com
Timna Woollard timnawoollard.com

SUPPLIERS

BATHROOMS
Aston Matthews astonmatthews.co.uk
Catchpole & Rye catchpoleandrye.com
Clearwater clearwaterbaths.com
Holloways of Ludlow hollowaysofludlow.com
London Encaustic londonencaustic.com
Victorian Plumbing victorianplumbing.co.uk
William Holland williamholland.com

CERAMICS
Lydia Hardwick lydiahardwick.co.uk
Anissa Kermiche anissakermiche.com

DOORS AND WINDOWS
Crittall crittall-windows.co.uk

FURNITURE
Another Country anothercountry.com
B&B Italia bebitalia.com
Cassina cassina.com
Dirk Van der Kooij dirkvanderkooij.com
Eichholtz eichholtz.com
Ercol ercol.com
Gervasoni gervasoni1882.com
Herman Miller hermanmiller.com
Howe London howelondon.com
Ikea ikea.com
Knoll knoll-int.com
Ligne Roset ligne-roset.com
Malgorzata Bany malgorzatabany.com
Pinch pinchdesign.com
Rose Uniacke Interiors roseuniacke.com
Rossi di Albizzate rossidialbizzate.it
Rupert Bevan rupertbevan.com
Soane Britain soane.co.uk
Tonelli Design tonellidesign.com
Trove thetrove.co.uk
Varier x Ingrid Bredholt varieringridbredholt.
varierfurniture.com
Vielle + Frances vielleandfrances.com

KITCHENS
DeVol devolkitchens.co.uk
Plain English plainenglishdesign.co.uk

LIGHTING

Cristina Celestino cristinacelestino.com
CTO Lighting ctolighting.co.uk
Dyke & Dean dykeanddean.com
edit58 edit58.com
Esperia Luci esperialuci.com
Flos flos.com
Isamu Noguchi noguchi.org
Kelly Wearstler kellywearstler.com
Matilda Goad matildagoad.com
Ochre ochre.net
Rose Uniacke Interiors roseuniacke.com
Soane Britain soane.co.uk
Tamasine Osher tamasineosher.com
Tom Dixon tomdixon.net

PAINT AND WALLPAPER

Adam Bray adambray.info
Ben Pentreath pentreath-hall.com
Cole & Son cole-and-son.com
Craig & Rose craigandrose.com
Deborah Bowness deborahbowness.com
Dedar dedar.com
Designers Guild designersguild.com
Divine Savages divinesavages.com
Edward Bulmer Natural Paint
   edwardbulmerpaint.co.uk
Farrow & Ball farrow-ball.com
Fromental fromental.co.uk
GP & J Baker gpjbaker.com
Graham & Brown grahambrown.com
Harlequin harlequin.sandersondesigngroup.com
House of Hackney houseofhackney.com
KOI Colour Studio koifargestudio.no
Little Greene littlegreene.com
Mònica Subidé for Soler soler.co.uk/pages/wallpaper-
   soler-home
Morris & Co. morrisandco.sandersondesigngroup.com
Ottoline ottoline.co.uk
Paint & Paper Library paintandpaperlibrary.com
Papers and Paints papersandpaints.co.uk
Phillip Jeffries phillipjeffries.com
Pierre Frey pierrefrey.com
Pip Studio pipstudio.com
Poodle & Blonde poodleandblonde.com
Pure & Original pure-original.com
Sanderson sandersondesigngroup.com
Woodchip & Magnolia woodchipandmagnolia.co.uk

RUGS AND TEXTILES

Abraham Moon & Sons moons.co.uk
Andrew Martin andrewmartin.co.uk
Bennison Fabrics bennisonfabrics.com
Colefax & Fowler colefax.com
Colville colvilleofficial.com
House of Hackney houseofhackney.com
Melin Tregwynt melintregwynt.co.uk
Mulberry mulberry.com
The Rug Company therugcompany.com
Vanderhurd vanderhurd.com

TILES

Bert & May bertandmay.com
Ca' Pietra capietra.com
Fired Earth firedearthcom
Lapicida lapicida.com
Maison Bahya maison-bahya.com
Marrakech Design marrakechdesign.se
Neisha Crosland neishacrosland.com
New Ravenna newravenna.com
Surface View surfaceview.co.uk
UK Architectural Heritage uk-heritage.co.uk

DESTINATIONS

The Craftsman's Cottage
Semley Lodge, Semley, Wiltshire SP7 9AU
thecraftsmanscottage.com

Deans Court
Deans Court Lane, Wimborne, Dorset BH21 1EE
deanscourt.org

Kingshill Farmhouse
Elmley Nature Reserve, Kingshill Farm,
Isle of Sheppey, Kent ME12 3RW
elmleynaturereserve.co.uk

Spinks Nest
Kings Street, Hunworth, Norfolk NR24 2EH
spinksnest.com

Sunbury Antiques Market
Kempton Park Racecourse, Sunbury-on-Thames,
Surrey TW16 5AQ
Sandown Park Racecourse, Esher, Surrey KT10 9AJ
sunburyantiques.com

INDEX

A

Aarnio, Eero 73
Abraham Moon & Sons (rugs/textiles) 168
Al-Bader, Alex and Mishari 17, 52, 138, 166
Albert, Prince 13
Alhambra (Andalusia, Spain) 206
Allen, Linda 7, 84, 160
Anderson, Wes 124
Andrew Martin (rugs/textiles) 95
Another Country (furniture) 168
Arbuthnott, Kate (interiors) 102
Art Deco 219
Art Nouveau 13, 168
Arts and Crafts 22, 38, 151, 168
Ashmolean Museum (Oxford, UK) 187
Aston Matthews (bathrooms) 194
Azagury-Partridge, Solange 7, 44, 111, 128, 160

B

B&B Italia (furniture) 60
Bannister, Amanda 168–9
Bany, Malgorzata (furniture) 24, 78
Barton, Jo 102, 115, 134–7, 206, 218–19
Baughman, Milo 60
Beeton, Isabella 83, 84
    Mrs Beeton's Every Day Cookery and
    Housekeeping (1890) 83
Bennison Fabrics (rugs/textiles) 166
Berdoulat (interiors) 92, 116, 119
Berryman, Jo 18, 49, 58, 72–5, 87, 88–9, 190, 198
Bert & May (tiles) 31, 128
Boesen, Viggo 104
Bowness, Deborah (paint/wallpaper) 163, 165, 171
Bray, Adam (paint/wallpaper) 59
Brown, Sarah 122
Bruce, Samantha 155, 162–5, 217
Buckingham Palace (London, UK) 160
Burleigh Pottery 119
Bux, Danielle 17, 18–21, 49
BWArchitects 17, 64, 104

C

Ca' Pietra (tiles) 207
Carlisle, Louise 92
Cassina (furniture) 78
Castiglioni, Achille and Pier Giacomo 24
Catchpole & Rye (bathrooms) 190
Celestino, Cristina (lighting) 188
Chambers, Lucinda 7, 49, 70–1
Chandler, Leanne 102, 115, 140–3, 160, 190, 202–5
Chandler, Luke 140, 142
Chinoiserie 156
Clarence & Graves (interiors) 32
Clearwater (bathrooms) 188

Cole & Son (paint/wallpaper) 160
Colefax & Fowler (rugs/textiles) 166
Colville (rugs/textiles) 70
The Craftsman's Cottage 168–9
Craig & Rose (paint/wallpaper) 59
Crittall (doors/windows) 76, 78, 124
Crosland, Neisha (tiles) 207
CTO Lighting 73
Cunningham, Tricia (interiors) 217

D

Daudy, Kate 224
Deans Court 122
Dearle, John Henry 168
Dedar (paint/wallpaper) 27
De Morgan, William 13, 184, 206
Designers Guild (paint/wallpaper) 28, 228
DeVol (kitchens) 124
Dickens, Charles 44, 224
    Our Mutual Friend (1865) 44
Dirk Van der Kooij (furniture) 96
Divine Savages (paint/wallpaper) 171
Dixon, Tom (lighting) 28, 43
Duggan, Tiffany 155, 156–9
Dyke & Dean (lighting) 165

E

Eames, Charles and Ray 220, 232
eBay 166
Edis, Robert 151, 152, 155
    Decoration and Furniture of Town Houses (1881)
    151
edit58 (lighting) 101
Edward Bulmer Natural Paint (paint/wallpaper) 59
Eichholtz (furniture) 51
Ellis, Jolene 124
Ercol (furniture) 90, 227
Esperia Luci (lighting) 188

F

Farrow & Ball (paint/wallpaper) 32, 51, 58, 59, 90, 95,
    98, 101, 163, 193, 219, 220
Field Day Studio (interiors) 102, 115, 128, 134, 190,
    206, 219
Fired Earth (tiles) 31, 207
Flos (lighting) 24, 222
Fornasetti (interiors) 160
Frith, William Powell 43
Fromental (paint/wallpaper) 156
Fournet, Emilie (interiors) 34, 94–5, 138, 155

G

Gervasoni (furniture) 78
Glover, Anna (interiors) 172

Goad, Matilda (lighting) 101
Godsal, Sam 34, 49, 92
Goldsmith, Sheherazade 232–3
Gordon, Rebecca 166
Gothic Revival 13, 14
Gowing, Josh 27, 188
Gowing, Scarlett 17, 26–7, 43, 83, 187, 188–9
GP & J Baker (paint/wallpaper) 166
Graham & Brown (paint/wallpaper) 170
Graves, Chris 17, 32–3, 68, 102, 115, 124–7, 234
Great Exhibition (1851) 8

H

Haas, Christian 138, 187, 234
Hardwick, Lydia (ceramics) 119
Harlequin (paint/wallpaper) 177
Heaton, Sarah 190
Herman Miller (furniture) 78
Holloways of Ludlow (bathrooms) 203
Horncastle & Son 43
House of Hackney (paint/wallpaper, rugs/textiles)
    163, 165, 170, 171, 187, 193, 194
Howark Design (interiors) 122, 234
Howe London (furniture) 67
Huc, Emily 144, 190, 234

I

Ikea (furniture) 96, 166, 227
The Illustrated London News 151

J

Jen Talbot Design (interiors) 213
Jewell, Lisa 34, 92
J.L. Mott Iron Works 111, 112
Jones, Owen 206

K

Kellie, Nikki 128
Kermiche, Anissa (ceramics) 51
Kingshill Farmhouse 184
Knoll (furniture) 27, 188
KOI Colour Studio (paint/wallpaper) 222
Koulouras, Nikos 34, 87
Krassa, Afroditi 34
Kristiansen, Kai 96

L

Lapicida (tiles) 207
Leek Embroidery Society 38
Leighton House (London, UK) 206
Lenka 200
Liberty 43
Ligne Roset (furniture) 27
Lineker, Gary 18

Lion in Frost 62
Little Greene (paint/wallpaper) 36, 38, 59, 70, 115, 196, 227
London Encaustic (bathrooms) 203
Loquet 232

M

Mackintosh, Charles Rennie 232
Magistretti, Vico 104
Magowan, Helen 155, 172–5
Maison Bahya (tiles) 31, 207
Maison Jansen 67, 220
Maple & Co. 151
Marrakech Design (tiles) 207
Maw & Co. 14
Mayoralgo, Juan de 13
McEwan, Simone 24, 78
Mehydene, Lisa 96, 151
Melin Tregwynt (rugs/textiles) 168
Memphis Group 220
Michaelis Boyd (architects) 17, 24–5, 76–9, 92, 111, 198
Minton, Herbert 13, 14
Mintons 30
Morris & Co. (paint/wallpaper) 160, 166, 168, 170, 171
Morris, William 13, 38, 152
Mouille, Serge 232
Mulberry (rugs/textiles) 101
Mulryan, Mary 9, 98–9, 138, 234
Musik, Fred 155, 177

N

National Portrait Gallery (London, UK) 187
Navone, Paola 78
Nelson, George 78
New Ravenna (tiles) 207
Nice Projects (interiors) 24, 78
Noguchi, Isamu (lighting) 78, 222

O

Ochre (lighting) 104
Oetzmann & Co. 213
Orton, Dr Thomas 160
Osborne House (Isle of Wight, UK) 13
Osher, Tamasine (lighting) 102
Ottoline (paint/wallpaper) 177

P

Paint & Paper Library (paint/wallpaper) 224
Palace of Westminster (London) 13
Panchamia, Deepa (artist) 172
Panton, Mrs J.E. 43, 52
Papers and Paints (paint/wallpaper) 59
Parker, Susannah 87, 90–1, 115, 128, 177, 187, 192–5, 224

Patrick Lewis Architects 175
Paulin, Pierre 9
Pentreath, Ben (paint/wallpaper) 170, 171
Perez, Ana 96, 144, 196–7
Phillip Jeffries (paint/wallpaper) 60
Pierre Frey (paint/wallpaper) 73, 151
Pinch (furniture) 168
Pip Studio (paint/wallpaper) 190
Plain English (kitchens) 92, 198
Platner, Warren 27, 188
Pollock, Charles 27
Poodle & Blonde (paint/wallpaper) 171
Pugin, A.W.N. (Augustus Welby Northmore) 13
Pure & Original (paint/wallpaper) 222

Q

Quadrille 7
Queen Anne Revival 58

R

Ridge & Furrow (interiors) 196
Rietveld, Gerrit 78
Robin Cooper (stained glass) 18
Rossi di Albizzate (furniture) 220
Rowan Plowden, Francesca (interiors) 184
Rowley, John 200
The Rising Sun pub (Bath, UK) 116
The Rug Company (rugs/textiles) 28, 67
Rupert Bevan (furniture) 104
Russell, Lucy 68, 102, 177, 183, 224

S

Saarinen, Eero 104
Sanderson (paint/wallpaper) 92, 170, 171
Scheele's Green 160
Shanks & Co. 183, 184
Sharp, Suzanne 9, 17, 28–9, 44, 52, 64, 67, 115, 166, 198, 213, 228
Silber & Fleming 13
Sims, George 83
Sloan, Annie 9, 49, 54–7, 59
Soames, Flora (interiors) 13, 49, 60–3
Soane Britain (furniture/lighting) 62, 67, 89
Soler 166
Sottsass, Ettore 187
Spinks Nest 166, 196–7
Spitfire factory 144
Storey, Robert 96
Subidé, Mònica (paint/wallpaper) 166
Sunbury Antiques Market 101
Surface View (tiles) 187, 206
Sykes, Pandora 49, 50–1, 151, 177, 224

T

10 Downing Street 22
Matteo Thun 220
Tonelli Design (furniture) 232
Trove (furniture) 156
Turner, Mairead 36–9, 177, 226–7
Twyford 184, 190

U

UK Architectural Heritage (tiles) 31
Uniacke, Rose (lighting) 24, 67

V

Valencia, Lisa 144, 200–1
Vanderhurd (rugs/textiles) 60
Varier x Ingrid Bredholt (furniture) 147
The Vawdrey House (interiors) 68, 115, 130–3
Vernon, Collette 14, 220–1
Veronese, Paolo 206
    Happy Union (1575) 206
Victoria and Albert Museum (London, UK) 187
Victorian Plumbing (bathrooms) 194
Victoria, Queen 7, 13, 160
Vielle + Frances (furniture) 156
Von Arx, Leanne 102, 112, 152
Von Hurter, Sandra Barrio 68, 100–1, 187, 224, 228

W

Walter, Basil 64, 104
Ward, Fleur 228
Wardle, Elizabeth 38
Wardle, Thomas 38
Wearstler, Kelly (lighting) 213
Wegner, Hans J. 92, 96
White, Annabel 7, 17, 43, 49, 64–7, 87, 104–7, 177
White Arrow (interiors) 128, 138
White, Jos 64–7, 104–7, 214
William Andrus 73
William Holland (bathrooms) 184, 200
Williams, Neri 116
Williams, Patrick 115, 116–21
William Woollams & Co. 44
Wilson, Steph 87, 206
Woodchip & Magnolia (paint/wallpaper) 171
Woollard, Timna (interiors) 104
Wright, Hannah 83, 228

Y

Yanagi, Sori 187

Z

Zanelli, Siri 115, 146–7, 198, 222–3
Z He 183, 198

ACKNOWLEDGMENTS

This book is dedicated to Philip Leevers, with thanks and love; and to Linda and David Smith, with thanks for all your love and support.

A huge thank you to the homeowners who welcomed us into their beautiful homes: we really appreciate the help and generosity of each and every one of you. We are also indebted to the interior designers, architects and creative people – and their representatives – who shared their projects with us.

At Thames & Hudson, many thanks to Fleur Jones for believing in our idea and bringing us into the Thames & Hudson fold. A big thank you to Elain McAlpine for her insight and expertise – and her endless patience as she steered us through the process of producing an interiors book. Our gratitude to everyone else in the Thames & Hudson team who played a role in bringing this book to life, including Jane Cutter, Tristan de Lancey, Daniele Roa and Clare Turner, and to Tim Balaam and Kate Sclater of Hyperkit.

Thank you to Susannah Marriott and Nikki Kellie for their expert advice, and to all the magazine and newspaper supplement editors we are lucky enough to work for regularly. A special mention for Mary Weaver from Jo for giving me my first interiors feature commission and for introducing me to Rachael. From Rachael, a special thank you to Rupert Thomas: thank you for hiring me all those years ago and for your unstinting support. Thank you to Monica Mascheroni, our brilliant Italian agent. Thanks also to Alison Cavanagh, who styled at Christian Haas's home, and Marcia Morgan who styled at Sam Godsal's home.

Last but not least, thank you to our families for giving us so much support while we worked on this book.

ABOUT THE AUTHOR AND PHOTOGRAPHER

Jo Leevers is an interiors writer, stylist and author. She has written for *World of Interiors*, *Homes & Gardens*, *Livingetc*, *Elle Decoration* and *Country Living*, the *Times*, *Telegraph* and *Observer* newspapers, and magazines in Europe, the US and Australia.
joleevers.com

Rachael Smith is an interiors photographer whose work appears regularly in *House & Garden*, *World of Interiors*, *Elle Decoration*, *Homes & Gardens*, *Architectural Digest* and magazines in Asia and Europe, and the *Times*, *Observer* and *Telegraph*. Her books include *London Shopfronts* (2021) and *Dungeness: Coastal Architecture* (2022). *rachaelsmith.net*

On the cover: Front Old and new elements come together in Christopher Lian's London apartment; *Back, left to right* Wallpaper in 'Seaweed' brightens up a cosy bedroom; a kitchen by Howark Design in a former Bermondsey tannery; 'Troop' wallpaper by House of Hackney in Devon

First published in the United Kingdom in 2023 by Thames & Hudson Ltd, 181A High Holborn, London WC1V 7QX

First published in the United States of America in 2023 by Thames & Hudson Inc., 500 Fifth Avenue, New York, New York 10110

Reprinted 2025

Victorian Modern: A Design Bible for the Victorian Home
© 2023 Thames & Hudson Ltd, London
Text © 2023 Jo Leevers
Photographs © 2023 Rachael Smith
(except as listed on p. 237)

Designed by Hyperkit
Cover design by Thames & Hudson Ltd, London

British Library Cataloguing-in-Publication Data
A catalogue record for this book is available from the British Library

Library of Congress Control Number 2022945748

ISBN 978-0-500-02404-1

Printed and bound in China by 1010 Printing International Ltd

MIX
Paper | Supporting responsible forestry
FSC® C016973
www.fsc.org

Be the first to know about our new releases, exclusive content and author events by visiting
thamesandhudson.com
thamesandhudsonusa.com
thamesandhudson.com.au